HOW TO
ZOOM
YOUR
ROOM

HOW TO ZOOM YOUR ROOM

Room Rater's Ultimate Style Guide

CLAUDE TAYLOR & JESSIE BAHREY

ILLUSTRATIONS BY CHRIS MORRIS

VORACIOUS

Little, Brown and Company
New York | Boston | London

Copyright © 2022 by Jessie Bahrey and Claude Taylor
Illustrations copyright © 2022 by Chris Morris

Hachette Book Group supports the right to free expression and the value of
copyright. The purpose of copyright is to encourage writers and artists to produce
the creative works that enrich our culture.

The scanning, uploading, and distribution of this book without permission
is a theft of the author's intellectual property. If you would like permission to
use material from the book (other than for review purposes), please contact
permissions@hbgusa.com. Thank you for your support of the author's rights.

Voracious / Little, Brown and Company
Hachette Book Group
1290 Avenue of the Americas, New York, NY 10104
littlebrown.com

First Edition: June 2022

Voracious is an imprint of Little, Brown and Company, a division of Hachette
Book Group, Inc. The Voracious name and logo are trademarks of Hachette Book
Group, Inc.

The publisher is not responsible for websites (or their content) that are not owned
by the publisher.

The Hachette Speakers Bureau provides a wide range of authors for speaking
events. To find out more, go to hachettespeakersbureau.com or call (866) 376-
6591.

Design by Bonni Leon-Berman

Photography/artwork by Chris Morris

The Oval Office images on pages 102, 104, and 107 are based on diagrams from
"The Evolution of the Oval Office Décor" by American Home Shield, www.ahs.
com/home-matters/resources/the-evolution-of-the-oval-office-decor/.

The images on pages, 37, 40, 41, 42, and 43 were reproduced from images
available on Wikimedia Commons

ISBN 978-0-316-42812-5
LCCN 2021948118

10 9 8 7 6 5 4 3 2 1

WOR

Printed in the United States of America

Contents

HOW TO
ZOOM
YOUR
ROOM

Introduction

As the COVID-19 pandemic brought the world to its knees in the spring of 2020, we all struggled to find a way to carry out our lives in this new reality. Working from home became the norm for many people. And, as most of us were spending most of our time at home, we watched more TV. The news we were watching became increasingly dire; as the numbers of deaths accelerated and infections dominated the news cycle, moments of humor and levity became precious.

The virus exposed inequalities and deep divisions in society, but one democratizing effect was that we got a chance to see how our favorite journalists, political pundits, and celebrities lived when not in a studio. We saw the art, décor, and "stuff," but also the messy rooms, rambunctious children, and photobombing pets. It was in this climate that Room Rater struck a collective nerve.

The Room Rater Twitter account began one Sunday in April 2020 as a way to have some fun doing exactly what many of us were already doing. Discussing our favorite political figures' and journalists' rooms was a welcome reprieve and a way to connect with people in a socially distanced way. We took it to another level and created an account that just rated the rooms using a 1–10 scale. We had no idea it would catch on like it did, but we realized by the end of the first week that we had something special. We found a way to combine useful advice and (generally) constructive criticism with political satire. As our follower count grew, many of our favorite talking heads began to have fun with our tweets, and those interactions became a daily event.

Room Rater quickly gained prominence with mentions in media, so that by the close of 2020 we even made the *Hollywood Reporter*'s annual list of "names" that had the greatest impact on popular culture. With all the attention, we decided to add a charitable element and started raising money for PPE for Native American communities.

Room Rater went viral for its satiric qualities, but it actually has real utility. As millions of people have adapted to our new forced reality, we've become accustomed to joining friends, celebrating birthdays, conducting work meetings, and having most other interactions via Skype or Zoom. As the pandemic continues into its second year, it's quite clear that Zooming and other new forms of communication will become a lasting reality. While we have vaccines and can see light at the end of the tunnel, many companies are realizing that working from home is cost-efficient. And many employees, when given the option to go back to the office or work remotely, are choosing the latter. As people continue to find virtual alternatives to face-to-face meetings, their rooms will continue to be seen, and Room Rater's helpful hints will be of use for a long time to come.

The Twitter account that began as a bit of fun and political satire grew very quickly. We now rate journalists from across the country, writers from every genre, sports figures, musicians, and actors—many of whom merrily engage with us on Twitter as they seek to improve their scores. All of this has broadened our reach. We have developed a unique position on social media as the arbiter or judge for all things related to a Zoom room's art, furnishings, décor, and taste. Zoom rooms look very different now than they did when we began, and this change appears to be here to stay.

We've never made any secret of the fact that we're not interior designers or decorators, and rating rooms was most definitely not our day job. However, after seeing hundreds of thousands of rooms, we've picked up a thing or two. We saw what worked and what didn't, and what our followers got excited about and what they didn't like. We saw how those with grand rooms, rooms that most of us can only aspire to, ruin their appearance with the height of the camera. We saw ingenious solutions for small, cramped spaces. We saw the very worst hostage video situations and the rooms with all the best elements plus the wow factor, and everything in between.

Our style guide is for everyone, from broadcasters to office workers to freelancers to teachers working from home. The tips we learned along the way can be applied anywhere video calls are made, from home offices to office offices. We offer simple, inexpensive, and easily achieved solutions to issues such as lighting, camera angles and heights, reflections, and distractions. Simple additions such as plants, pets, and even an appearance by a child or two can add warmth and a sense of camaraderie to any sterile conference call. We can help you nail the interview, earn the promotion, and impress your friends and family. The best news is that you won't require a large lottery win or a move to a new home. With a little bit of effort and savvy, we can help you make a Zoom room all-star—and not just on social media, but in the real world.

Setup Style #1
THE BASIC BOOKSHELF

The bookshelf is the foundational design element of many of the rooms seen on television, and this applies as well to our Zoom screens at home. Composing a visually appealing background is no longer a matter left to the political pundits and journalists of cable news. From parent-teacher conferences to book club meetings, nearly everyone now finds themselves broadcasting their homes to the outside world. A bookshelf can be done well or done poorly. When done right, it sends the message that you're well-read and are in the word business. People need to take you seriously; you have the knowledge to back up your thoughts.

The key here is what we call spacing, i.e., the distance between you and the bookshelves directly behind you. What you don't want to do is place yourself with your back or the back of your chair right up against the shelves. It creates a flat and uninteresting effect. Start with a foot of space behind you. Try two feet. Play with it. Do you want the individual titles to be legible? Do you want to underline the fact that you have All the Right Books behind you or do you want just the general aesthetic appeal of a wall of books? If you want the visual effect but don't want to get bogged down in title selection, then the more spacing the better.

So you have your bookshelves or bookcases directly behind you. You're going with about two feet of spacing between you and the books. But you're not done yet. Books are great, we are pro-book, but the question is: Do you go for an all-book look? We say the answer is an emphatic no. You need a few details. Something to break things up. Vases. Plants. Small potted succulents are a great low-maintenance way to go. Almost any item from our list of Top 25 Décor Items will work. But put something of yourself in there. A favorite knickknack. A souvenir from your travels, perhaps? That snow globe you picked up somewhere. Family photos. We don't recommend you overdo it, but filling some of the shelves' surface with objects other than books can be very effective.

A mistake people often make is leaving too much open space. We subscribe to an 80/20 rule. Remember this rule. Eighty percent of the actual shelf space should be filled with books. Twenty percent should be other than books: plants, vases, etc., as discussed above. What you must avoid doing is leaving shelves or large sections of shelves entirely empty. If this is a book setup, fill it with books.

Addendum:
The Nonbook Bookshelf Setup

Opinions differ on this one. Some feel that bookcases/bookshelves are made for books and should be used for that purpose only. We are not so absolutist on this. We find there are many well-thought-out setups using bookshelves that display a plethora of nonbook objects. While we don't recommend this approach, if it's done well and is what we refer to as well curated, it can be effective.

Angle

The book setup is the way to go for a large plurality of people. A simple change can take your bookshelf setup to another level. Try positioning yourself and set up the shot so the bookcase/shelf is at a sharp angle. By doing so, you create a shot with more depth. Try working with angle and adjusting the depth to find the most flattering shot for you and your setup.

The principal advantage you gain here is depth. By shooting

"down" your bookshelf, you're creating a sense of depth in relatively few feet. You can adjust the angle so that in addition to the shelves, you can incorporate a piece of artwork or furniture at the end or on the adjoining wall. This opens up a wide range of possibilities, depending on the space available.

Make sure you don't neglect lighting—you don't want the far end of your angled shelves to drift off into darkness.

If you're interested in calling attention to certain books, you'll want to make sure they're placed at the close end of the bookshelves, with the most clearly recognizable usually in view just off/over your left or right shoulder, depending on how you set up the shot.

ROOM RATER TOP TIPS

KEITH BALDREY CANADIAN JOURNALIST FROM GLOBAL TV

Amidst the gathering gloom of the COVID-19 pandemic, an unexpected bright spot emerged that simultaneously put a smile on people's faces and greatly improved their ability to communicate in new and unexpected ways.

That would be Room Rater, a social media sensation that combined deft wit, political knowledge, and some seriously good tips for looking good on camera while sitting at a desk or computer.

I credit Room Rater for convincing me to drop my "in jail" look (the bars on the window behind me made it seem like I was reporting from a jail cell; or so Room Rater insinuated on Twitter when they asked if I needed bail money) and adopt some plants and books. I went from an initial 5/10 grade to the coveted 10/10 mark. They also inspired me with the idea to showcase local authors by placing their books on my bookcase for all to see.

I for one cannot wait for this pandemic to end. But here's hoping Room Rater continues its charming existence long afterward.

— Keith Baldrey

Freestyle

Subject

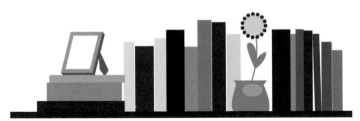

20/80

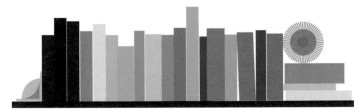

Color-coded

All About Books

If you are using books as part of or the main focus of your setup, there are several issues to consider, such as display, topic, and format. Are fiction and nonfiction mixed? Are hardcovers mixed with paperbacks? Should you get the same fifteen or so titles that most of the Inside the Beltway types seem to favor? (See "More About Books: *The Power Broker*.")

Organizing Your Books

There are a lot of bookshelf organizing options. Most of them are good. But a couple are bad (we'll get to those in a bit).

1. Freestyle. Stuff your books in that shelf any old way. Who cares? We like books. We like people who like books, and we like rooms with books. Slide a few volumes on top. They don't have to look perfectly organized, nor should they. Have a lot of books? Small apartment? We are okay with double rows. Do what you want. They are your books.

2. Organize by subject, but let's not be too precise. All the biographies go together. Fiction is one section. Nonfiction is separate. Broad categories. Look at the big picture. They will overlap, and that's fine.

3. Organize by author within categories. Takes a little more time and is more for those who desire a higher bit of order in their life, but it's quite satisfying if it fits your personality and lifestyle.

DR. PETER HOTEZ — CO-DIRECTOR, CENTER FOR VACCINE DEVELOPMENT, TEXAS CHILDREN'S HOSPITAL

More About Books

We like bookends and feel their decline in popularity is unfortunate. Bookends can help communicate a sense of style. They can be plain and purely about function. Or they can display more personality and be a décor point. We are decidedly pro-bookend. They should be considered.

Another consideration: vertical versus horizontal stacking. Room Rater has a bias here, which we're going to be open about. We prefer vertically stacked books. Mostly. Books are meant to be stacked and organized vertically, with the book's spine running perpendicular to the shelf it's on. That is not to say some horizontally stacked books are unacceptable. It's a question of ratio. How many horizontal to vertical.

There are exceptions. It is acceptable to use a short stack of horizontal books to function as bookends at the end of a shelf. However, this can be overdone and in most cases, the use of a bookend or three is preferable.

Another exception is where large-scale books such as coffee table, children's, and art books won't physically fit vertically. It is perfectly fine and expected that these will be stacked horizontally.

What is unacceptable and looks entirely staged is short stack after short stack of horizontal books, when one long row of vertically shelved books would do. It looks false and is not a useful way to access books.

That said, up to about 25 percent of books stacked horizontally/serving as bookends will pass muster if you deem it necessary. More than about this ratio and you start sending the signal that your books are for the show, not for the know.

Book Rules
What Not to Do

Of course, excessive horizontal stacking pales in comparison to the ultimate bookshelf blunder. Lives have been lost, blood has been spilled, and families have been torn apart over this matter: the dreaded color-coding of books.

Folks tend to have strong opinions on color-coding, and we're no exception. If you color-code your books, you should stop. Some will argue it's attractive and "pretty." Fundamentally, it treats books as primarily decorative objects rather than vessels of our knowledge and culture. It undervalues books and sends the message that neither books nor their owners are to be taken too seriously.

We at Room Rater are opposed to the color-coding of books. We are against it, but we recognize there are perfectly lovely people who disagree. We are right. They are wrong.

As an aside, removing a dust jacket from a hardcover—especially a valuable first edition—reduces its monetary value by about half.

Exceptions do exist. Having an entire book series or collection of the same color is not considered color-coding.

For Authors

ADAM SCHIFF   (D) CALIFORNIA

You wrote a book and you have every right to be proud of your achievement. Now you need to promote it on Zoom. One copy, cover forward, is the best approach.

We look askance at multiple copies of the same book. It looks a little overzealous and a tad desperate. Whether stacked ver-

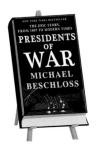

tically or horizontally, we really only want to see one copy of your book. But that book we do want to see. It should be close enough to your foreground so that the title is legible to the viewer. Placing it on a small easel can be effective. Simply having the cover forward as the lone book on your shelf is another common and effective way to go.

As serious an issue as the color-coding of books is, that is not the worst mistake you can make.

The worst mistake you can make is to display your books pages first.

We repeat, the worst thing you can do is to display a book with the spine in and the pages out. We're told this trend be-

gan with high-end interior decorators sharing an inside joke that got away from them. Don't do this. You will be made fun of. You will also deserve it.

JONATHAN CAPEHART · *THE SUNDAY SHOW WITH JONATHAN CAPEHART*

One of the two times I left journalism, I went into public relations. I always told clients that if a reporter came to interview them; "Your office tells a story about you." Luckily, I didn't have to curate my bookcases too much when I started doing TV from home. The objects reflected our design tastes. Adding the flowers was my husband's brilliant idea.

— Jonathan Capehart

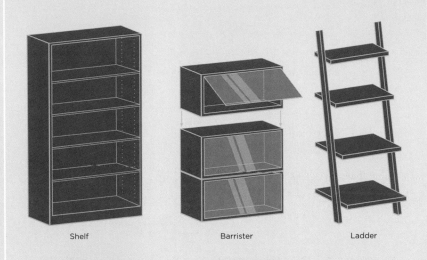

Shelf

Barrister

Ladder

Corner

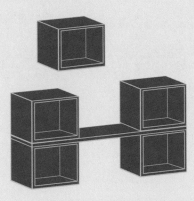

Modular

Bookshelf Styles

Shelf bookcases: Can be freestanding or built into a wall and can be open or closed in the back. They can be stacked or built up with other units. They can be metal, wood, or plastic.

Portable (barrister) bookcases: Originally designed for barristers in England to transport all their law books from one chamber to another, these bookcases contain separate shelf units that can be moved individually. They can also serve to protect the books within.

Ladder bookcases: Freestanding or leaning against a wall, the shelves resemble a ladder, with decreasing shelf size from the bottom shelf up. This is a great alternative for smaller spaces.

Corner bookcases: Great for small spaces and available in many shapes and styles, these are also great for rooms with unused corners. This will remove clutter and make the space look clean.

Modular: Basically, these are display cubes of various materials that can be used individually or in groups. They can be deployed in various groupings and can be assembled horizontally or vertically depending on your space.

More About Books

The Power Broker

B y now, you've made one of your most important background decisions. Books or no books. You are going with
books. It's a solid approach. Not really cutting-edge, but tried
and true. Dependable. Sometimes, old school works. Why not
embrace it? For the sake of discussion, we're going to assume
you've already decided whether your bookshelf, row of books,
or even entire wall of books (bookwall in these pages) is going
to be directly behind you, at an angle behind you, or against the
back wall. All of these choices can work well if done thought-
fully. As with many things, details count. If you've decided that
your books will be against the back wall, you're going more for
the overall aesthetic effect of a bookcase/bookwall, and we
need not concern ourselves with individual titles. However, it
will be important, as always, whether we can read the titles or
not, to scrupulously avoid color-coding.

This section will be for those who've chosen to have their books/bookshelf relatively close behind them or at an angle such that at least some of the titles are either legible or recognizable. This will be especially important if you're using a setup with only a few select books on an end table or what have you.

Now, it should be said that we're all for the free expression of ideas. You may simply not care which books are in your shot, and you may not be concerned with what others seeing your room may infer. So be it. But many of us will want to recognize that the books we read and own can communicate a great deal about who we are and the values we hold and the interests we pursue.

For those who have been part of the new Zooming experience or have watched it unfold, it will come as no surprise that certain books seem to have enormous popularity, especially among journalists, pundits, and opinion-makers. First and foremost, the single book you're most likely to see is Robert

Caro's 1,337-page epic story of politics and New York infrastructure, *The Power Broker*. That may be due in part to how wide the spine of the book is, but it also seems to convey the message that you have arrived. You made it. Or are at least reporting on it.

There are other oft-seen books. The postpresidency books by Bill Clinton and Barack Obama are on many shelves, as are presidential biographies in general and pretty much everything ever written by Doris Kearns Goodwin. Ron Chernow's *Grant* bio is the leader in this category. One trend your Room Raters have observed is that the book *Caste* by Isabel Wilkerson has been coming on strong and may have replaced *The Power Broker* as the most popular book to have, especially for those under forty.

Our position at Room Rater is that we don't much care what books you choose (although if you want easy points, check out our recommended reading list on the next page); just make the choice deliberate. Your decisions in this regard should be by design. We do not encourage anyone to buy books simply as background fodder, but we would prefer to see  the books you own arranged in a flattering way.

We like seeing important books from child-hood. On more than a few shelves, we've seen what appears to be a nearly complete set of dis-tinctive yellow-covered Nancy Drew mysteries.  We also appreciate classic book collections with recognizable spines, like the full set of Winston Churchill's history of World War II.

Room Rater
READING LIST

No collection of books could comprehensively document our cultural history or tell all the stories that deserve to be told. We hope, however, that this list does an honorable job of representing the time and place we live in, and gives some insight into how we got here. A stranger to our world would see in these pages the images that have become seared into our collective memory and would read about the moments in our past that toppled the dominoes whose fall has led us to today. If we hope to trace back to where we came from, who we are as a people, this is as good a place to start as any.

Nonfiction

Malick Sidibé: Photographs, Manthia Diawara (2004)

Hitchcock/Truffaut, François Truffaut and Alfred Hitchcock (1966)

AFRICANA, Kwame Anthony Appiah and Henry Louis Gates Jr. (1999)

August Sander: Citizens of the Twentieth Century—Portrait Photographs, 1892–1952 (1986)

Film Noir: An Encyclopedic Reference to the American Style, Alain Silver and Elizabeth Ward (1992)

Through a Window: My Thirty Years with the Chimpanzees of Gombe, Jane Goodall (1990)

The Murrow Boys: Pioneers on the Front Lines of Broadcast Journalism, Stanley Cloud and Lynne Olson (1996)

O'Neill: Son and Artist, Louis Sheaffer (1973)

Frederick Douglass: Prophet of Freedom, David W. Blight (2018)

A Bright Shining Lie: John Paul Vann and America in Vietnam, Neil Sheehan (1988)

These Truths: A History of the United States, Jill Lepore (2018)

King Leopold's Ghost: A Story of Greed, Terror, and Heroism in Colonial Africa, Adam Hochschild (1998)

The Right Stuff, Tom Wolfe (1979)

The Years of Lyndon Johnson Volume II: Means of Ascent, Robert Caro (1990)

Parting the Waters: America in the King Years 1954–63, Taylor Branch (1988)

The Swerve: How the World Became Modern, Stephen Greenblatt (2011)

The Metaphysical Club: A Story of Ideas in America, Louis Menand (2001)

Cultural Amnesia: Necessary Memories from History and the Arts, Clive James (2007)

Caste: The Origins of Our Discontents, Isabel Wilkerson (2020)

Chasing the Moon, Robert Stone and Allen Andres (2019)

Fiction

The Handmaid's Tale, Margaret Atwood (1985)

Midnight's Children, Salman Rushdie (1981)

Invisible Man, Ralph Ellison (1952)

Absalom, Absalom, William Faulkner (1936)

A Farewell to Arms, Ernest Hemingway (1929)

The Stories of John Cheever (1978)

The Things They Carried, Tim O'Brien (1990)

Song of Solomon, Toni Morrison (1977)

Gravity's Rainbow, Thomas Pynchon (1973)

The Collected Stories of Eudora Welty (1980)

The Underground Railroad, Colson Whitehead (2016)

One Hundred Years of Solitude, Gabriel García Márquez (1970)

Henderson the Rain King, Saul Bellow (1959)

American Pastoral, Philip Roth (1997)

The Mezzanine, Nicholson Baker (1988)

The Cyberiad, Stanislaw Lem (1974)

The Complete Stories, Flannery O'Connor (1971)

The Novels of Muriel Spark (1995)

Americanah, Chimamanda Ngozi Adichie (2013)

Swing Time, Zadie Smith (2016)

The Corrections, Jonathan Franzen (2001)

ROOM RATER TOP NO-NOS

DONNY DEUTSCH BRANDING & MARKETING EXPERT

No-No #1: Matchy-matchy

Avoid the too matchy-matchy.

There is symmetry and then there is too matchy-matchy. You'll know it when you see it. Here's a hint. Don't do more than one set of identical objects. Candles. Vases. What have you. Some may think it has a certain appeal, but in most cases it's distracting and unnecessary. It may seem like a good idea. It's not. Stop.

Art Styles

Art: No Warhol? No Worries.
No Picasso? No Problem.

One of the most fun aspects of getting to peek into people's homes during the pandemic has been being able to catch a glimpse of their art. The art we see is a reflection of your taste, and it always tells a story. We have seen paintings by Matisse and other famous artists. We have seen the magnificent art created by family or friends or local artists. We have seen kids' art (see "A Few of Our Favorite Things: Kids' Art"). Of course, fine art by famous artists is fun to look at, but we have seen reproductions that look great, fill the space well, and add color and sophistication to a room. By far the majority of the art we see is affordable for most people. Gallery-quality pieces are not necessary to fill those dreaded empty spaces on your walls. Just remember that larger pieces fill large spaces more easily than multiple small pieces, so keep the size of your rooms in mind.

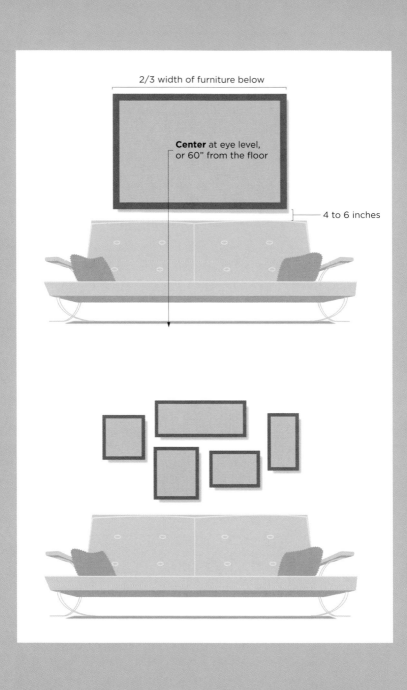

Now that you have the art, it needs to go on a wall. Getting the art hung at the right height is important and is governed by various criteria. The most basic and agreed-upon rule is to hang a single piece at eye level, with the piece's center sixty inches from the floor. If you live in a small space, a few inches lower will work better. Even when hanging multiple pieces, use the sixty-inch rule, but measure from the center of the array of pieces.

Hanging art: If you're hanging art above furniture, the lower edge of the piece in question should hang four to six inches above the furniture. When hanging art above a couch or headboard, the art looks best if it is two-thirds the width of the furniture. Try to avoid small pieces in these situations, or the art will get lost in the wall. There are lots of ways to fill a large space if a large piece is not available or desired. Several smaller ones arranged in a cool manner can work just as well or better. Three or five frames work better than four or six, but play with the different configurations—vertical, horizontal, or staggered. Have fun with it.

Something to avoid is the dreaded leaning art. Whether it is on the floor leaning against a wall or on a piece of furniture or a raised surface, this is just unnecessary. Leaning doesn't just diminish a piece's place in the room, it also makes the piece more

EUGENE ROBINSON | *THE WASHINGTON POST* ASSOCIATE EDITOR

Art brings a room to life because it satisfies some primal human need for beauty that predates civilization, much less Skype and Zoom. There are only two rules. First, choose good art rather than bad (it helps to marry a great artist). Second, be bold. Like the prehistoric postmodernists who painted Picassoesque bulls in the caves of Lascaux, or like the petroglyphic masters of Nazca who anticipated Keith Haring by a thousand years, make a visual statement that commands attention. You have to have faith that viewers will be riveted by your compelling words, and thus not distracted by your art. But you also have to be realistic enough to admit to yourself that once in a great while your reportage or analysis might be less than dazzling. So give the people something to look at. Let them see what you see, and feel what you feel, when the camera and the microphone are off. That knowledge forges a deeper connection. If a bookshelf is a window onto the mind, a picture is a window onto the soul.

— Eugene Robinson

difficult to see and can add to surface clutter. Plus, there is a safety factor, because it looks precarious and can be distracting. There are two exceptions to this no-no: if you have just moved into a new space and you don't have the proper tools to hang right now; or if the piece is new and you are determining where it will look best.

Some of our very favorite things to see on walls are vintage travel posters. These fit all the criteria of art; they tell a story, they fill empty wall spaces, and they add color and personality to any room. Originally, they were made to advertise travel and the travel industry. Before television was invented, posters were a major method of advertising. As air travel grew in popularity and more people were able to see faraway places, airlines and hotels began to put up posters designed to encourage people to book trips.

Over the years, travel posters became one of the most common kinds of collectibles, and they should take their rightful place in the world of art. They show exotic places and bright colors and look good on walls in their own right. Often they have significance and memories for their owner and can be a great conversation starter.

Much like travel posters, we view movie posters as art. They were designed to bring people into the theater to see a particular movie, and as the film industry grew, so did the quality of the movie advertising. The industry has evolved and moved online and to television for much of its advertising budget, so movie posters have become increasingly scarce. However, they are popular with collectors, and they make perfect sense on your walls. They are bright and eye-catching and tell a story.

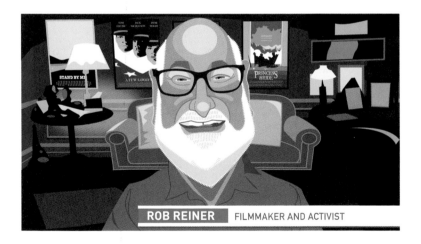

ROB REINER FILMMAKER AND ACTIVIST

CLOISONNÉ

JONATHAN ALLEN REPORTER, NBC NEWS

Cloisonné is a technique that creates designs on metal objects with colored material (like glass, gems, or enamel) that is then held in place by wire or metal strips. The small compartments, or cloisons, that hold the material remain visible after the item is finished.

This technique dates back to ancient Mesopotamia and Egypt, when it was used in jewelry, first with gems and then with enamel. The Byzantines, Chinese, Japanese, and Russians all adopted the technique and made it their own. In modern times, cloisonné is used for gifts, souvenirs, other ornamental objects, jewelry, and vases, like the one above. Over forty colors of enamel are used. Cloisonné pieces can be seen in galleries and museums all over the world. If you can obtain any piece, you must display it whenever you are able, including during video calls!

FINE ART PHOTOGRAPHY

Fine art photography is photography as art. It uses the camera to express an idea, thought, or emotion, much the same way as with painting and sculpture. The artist uses the camera as a tool to create this art, which is what they see, not to simply document the subject as the camera sees it.

Ansel Adams, Diane Arbus, and Henri Cartier-Bresson are just three famous artists of this genre. In the modern era, photography itself has become digitized and technical, and computers have changed the nature of fine art photography too. Artists can manipulate images even more and can communicate their messages more easily.

IMPRESSIONISM

Impressionism began in the late nineteenth century. Impressionist art is characterized by the use of small brush-strokes and an emphasis on light. These works convey an "impression" of the subject, as opposed to a realistic depiction. The work of Impressionist painters tended to use bright colors, which was a departure from previous, more conventional styles. The Impressionist painters make bold use of layers, showing yet more color below the surface.

Some of the more famous Impressionists were Claude Monet, Mary Cassatt, Henri Matisse, and Paul Cézanne. The Impressionist movement itself has endured over the years, likely because it emphasized modernism and led to later art movements throughout Europe.

POP ART

Put in simple terms, pop art uses objects from mass culture as subjects. In some ways, pop art can be seen as a revolt against traditional views of art in history

The pop art movement began in the mid-1950s in Britain and a few years later in the US. Although traditionalists were somewhat horrified at the subject matter of this new art, young artists were inspired by the world around them. Pop art can be viewed as an early form of postmodernism. Famous examples are, of course, Andy Warhol, Roy Lichtenstein, and Yayoi Kusama.

ABSTRACT ART

Abstract art can be thought of as nonrepresentational art, or art that has no reference to anything literal. Modern abstract art began in the early 1900s

and was considered radical and highly controversial in its time.

This art form has continued to be popular since its early days and is highly versatile. It exists in two- and three-dimensional pieces and can be made of many different materials and surfaces. There are subgenres, and abstract art can even be mixed with realistic art. Abstraction appeals to the curious and the rebels, and especially to the rule-breakers. Some well-known artists in this style are Jackson Pollock, Mark Rothko, Willem de Kooning, and Helen Frankenthaler.

SURREALISM

Surrealism is the artistic and philosophical movement established by French poet André Breton. In his 1924 manifesto, Breton raises the concept of a "super-reality." The surrealists believed that artistic creativity stems from the unconscious mind.

Surrealist art is distinguished by symbols and imagery meant to show ideas from the unconscious. It also by nature rejects conventional ideas and art forms. Some leading surrealist artists are Salvador Dalí, Frida Kahlo, Joan Miró, and Man Ray.

SEN. MAZIE HIRONO (D) HAWAII, JUDICIARY COMMITTEE

Living with art brings the all-important creative spirit into my life. My DC apartment is too small to display paintings or other large works, so I collected art quilts over the years, as they are more compact and easier to transport. These quilts, my video call backdrop, reflect my love of art. Several of the artists have recognized their quilts in these videos and have contacted me, a lovely surprise.

— Sen. Mazie Hirono

Another of the things we love to see is your kids' art. And we are not alone. Everyone loves to see it on walls, on shelves, or in some cases on fridges. As the pandemic dragged on, we started to see more children's art displayed in various rooms, and those became great moments of shared connection. Making it personal, adding that element of human warmth, can make a Zoom room come alive. What better way of doing that than proudly displaying art by your loved ones? It's not about proving your kid is the next Jackson Pollock, but about showing you are relatable and value your family.

ROOM RATER TOP TIPS

RICHARD ZUSSMAN REPORTER, BC LEGISLATURE

Be proud of your children and their talents will reward you far more than you can imagine. Kids' art allows for a connection to the audience, a window somehow into the lives of the person you see on television. I'm lucky my kids love to draw and paint. It adds a variety of styles and colors. We also worked on a locally themed drawing project bringing people into the guessing game of what picture would be next. It's also hard to find someone who doesn't love seeing a kid's drawing.

— Richard Zussman

Wall Treatment

Wall Color Is Art

One of the best-known rules of home renovation specialists is that a coat of paint is the most effective and inexpensive way to update a room. But walls can be so much more than an element to hang art on; if you choose the right color, the wall itself can become a work of art.

Slapping on a fresh coat of white paint will update and brighten, but it will not show off your personality or give a room the wow factor. Most people are intimidated by bright, bold hues. But the worst that can happen is that you will have to repaint. So take a leap and find something you love on the color wheel at your local paint store. Start with just one wall as an accent.

Here are a few simple tips on choosing wall color:

Keep in mind your existing furniture, rugs, décor, and art. Pick something that will accent or complement your existing color scheme. Unless your plan includes a more extensive renovation and new furnishings, you can develop a few options from existing items in the rooms you are going to paint—a vase or a throw, or a favorite piece of art. Remember to bring the paint chips home and take your time making your decision.

Think of how you want the room to feel. This of course is subjective, but some colors are more relaxing, energetic, or warm than others. The room you Zoom from will always be more interesting if it has some of your personality in it. The walls may not be able to talk, but they can complement or detract from how your room looks while you do the talking. You may want to try out one of our personal favorites, like a warm red, royal blue, or hunter green. Burnt orange still has appeal as well, but we are just talking wall color here.

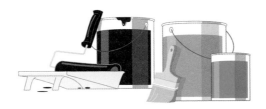

YAMICHE ALCINDOR NBC/MSNBC WASHINGTON CORRESPONDENT

Don't be scared of bold colors and adding the fun parts of your personality to your room. A good wall color can make your background shine and give you a beautiful canvas to add other designs. Take your time choosing. Order as many paint samples as your heart desires, because seeing the shade in person, next to your other room features, is key. I leaned into my love of pink and green, the colors of my sorority, Alpha Kappa Alpha, the first black sorority in the nation. I went through a zillion shades of green before landing on Sherwin-Williams's Grand Canal, a charming shade that complemented pale pink and gold accents. Also, think outside the box. I wanted plants without more tables so I hung them on the wall. I wanted a bookcase with spunk so I added pots next to my literary favorites.

— Yamiche Alcindor

The Great Wallpaper Comeback

Wallpaper dates back to the Renaissance, when the upper classes commonly hung large tapestries on their walls. These were so expensive that those who couldn't afford them created wallpaper to look like tapestries. Britain became the world's largest exporter, and there was even a wallpaper tax from 1712 to 1836. By the early twentieth century, wallpaper was everywhere as it became an affordable option in home decoration. While it had gone somewhat out of style (remember your aunt's yellowing walls) and came to be associated with dated décor, the rise of DIY home renovation television shows has helped reinvigorate its popularity. Wallpapering, just like painting, is a quick and inexpensive way to change the look of a room that most people can even do themselves.

Wallpaper can be as much a form of art or personal expression as paint. And much as choosing a bold paint color can be intimidating, wallpaper can cause anxiety. There are no real rules other than matching the size of the print pattern to the size of the room.

CHRIS KREBS
FORMER DIRECTOR, CYBERSECURITY AND
INFRASTRUCTURE SECURITY AGENCY

Before making the full commitment, we recommend pinning a strip on the intended wall for a day or so to see if you like it. You can also see how the paper looks in different light during the day. Vertical stripes will make the ceiling look higher; so will lighter backgrounds. The best place to start is by looking online or in home decorating magazines and then going to a physical store. There are lots of good YouTube videos on hanging techniques if you decide to do it yourself, but in either case, it's worth a try.

ROOM RATER TOP TIPS

MELISSA MURRAY NYU LAW PROFESSOR

I was once skeptical of wallpaper—it seemed like a relic from the 1970s (and really hard to remove). But a designer friend pushed me to give it a fresh look and I loved what I saw—bold, colorful patterns, whimsical prints, easy removal options make wallpaper a great way to add joy and personality to your space. If you're hesitant, consider using it for an accent wall (that's how I started), or as the interior lining for bookcases, or in a powder room. Once you start, you'll be hooked.

— Melissa Murray

Covid Cabins

The origins of this category on Room Rater began when the reality of the pandemic hit and most people went into some sort of lockdown. Some people had a choice: head for the hills or the mountains. The more well-to-do went to the Hamptons. Many who had a "summer place" went there. And thus, the "covid cabin" was born. We note, most folks do not have that luxury. For some who did, knotty pine replaced white walls and bookcases.

We like them all. Log cabins, beach houses, cottages, forest and mountain cabins. At least for us, rustic chic, if done right, never goes out of style. If you are lucky enough to be staying or living in such a space, embrace the opportunity and go all in. Choose a theme/color scheme and décor accordingly. And flaunt it. The same rules apply to covid cabins, beach houses, and hotels, and these are, for all intents and purposes, your room. However, no one expects you to carry around your own art, plants, and perfect karate-chopped pillows when you are traveling for business or pleasure.

Even if your temporary housing situation is minimal, you can still move around some small furniture to make your

Zoom call as good as it can be. Check for the spot with the best light. Move around décor to show the best in your shot. You can switch the art around too, unless it's chained to the wall. The hardest part will be remembering where everything went after the call. We suggest taking a photo before moving everything around. No one will ever know.

NOEL CASLER   COMEDIAN AND PODCASTER

My Zoom mise en place is simple but meaningful. Since I am most likely going to be ranting about current affairs (in hopefully a humorous fashion) and revealing "secrets" from my years on the road in the music industry and live television, I like to have a setting that helps ground me. I want my room to have the calming feeling of a cabin in the woods that you can't wait to return to after a long tour bus ride. I have a hand-built stone fireplace made with rocks from the river behind my house in upstate New York—horse country. The wooden floors were also put in by hand. I like to

(cont.)

include a guitar or two that I have collected on the road. David Crosby, Jackson Browne, and Stephen Stills all taught me what to look for in great guitars—we would often spend days off on tour scouring local guitar shops when I was their road manager. A treasure like that in my Zoom frame reminds me that the only way to truly communicate is with love and harmony. Keeping it simple and true to yourself is the way to go for me. I have about twenty-five years' worth of backstage passes that I once thought of hanging nonchalantly in the background, but if I had, you probably wouldn't be reading this now. Being in the Room Rater 10/10 club is quite an honor and I look forward to seeing many more folks reach these lofty heights.

— Noel Casler

BEST USE OF SMALL SPACE

In many cities, urban sprawl has necessitated a shift from single-dwelling detached homes to town houses, condominiums, and apartments. This trend has long been in motion and is unlikely to slow anytime soon. There are well-established tricks to make a small space appear larger, and here are a few we have seen that work well:

1. Mirrors make rooms look larger. This is a trick that real estate agents use all the time when taking videos and photos

of properties they want to sell. Mirrors placed near windows will reflect light and can make a room appear to have more windows.

2. Using clean lines and simple shapes for your furnishings and décor will also make your space look bigger. There are many "condo-sized" options available for furniture that are far more appropriate and will look better than standard sizes. Furniture that is low to the floor will make your ceiling appear higher.

3. It's easy for a small space to look cluttered, so concentrate on a "less is more" strategy. Pick your favorite elements and use them as a base to build on.

4. Get the lighting off the floor. When possible, mount lighting on the walls and ceiling rather than using floor lamps or eating up precious space with table and desk lamps.

5. In the case of a very small room, a neutral tone on the walls will make the room appear larger than bright colors.

6. Organization is key in small spaces. Having furniture with built-in storage will help minimize clutter and keep things looking airy and clean. There are also closet organizers that work well.

7. Pick a color scheme and go for tones/shades in the same color family. This will look less busy and more relaxing.

8. While flooring that is the same throughout a room or house creates the illusion of space and flow, small rugs can actually make a room look smaller than it is. A larger rug can add an impression of size.

9. Like mirrors, glass-topped tables can make small spaces appear larger. Two smaller tables instead of one larger one will also help.

10. Most of us know the rules for the perfect height to hang art, but in small spaces, hanging it higher than you normally would will also make your space look larger.

11. Shelves can be your friend. We love "floating shelves," and these can also add precious space while keeping floor clutter to a minimum.

JONATHAN LEMIRE POLITICO/MSNBC JOURNALIST

It was a plain brick wall and there was only one nail.

But that was okay, I only needed to hang one thing. As the pandemic reached our shores, it became clear: at a time of fear and tumult, the nation needed an image of a comeback story, an image of good triumphing over evil.

An image of Alex Rodriguez getting punched in the face.

I'm an obsessive Boston Red Sox fan and a moment that I will cherish forever was the game against the hated New York Yankees in 2004 when the Sox catcher, Jason Varitek, smacked A-Rod in the mouth during a brawl.

The Sox later won that game in dramatic fashion and, soon after, turned their season around. Once in the play-offs, they became the first baseball team ever—ever!—to overcome a 3–0 series deficit and, all the sweeter, did so against the Yankees, a team that had owned us for decades. We capped off the season with our first World Series title in eighty-six years.

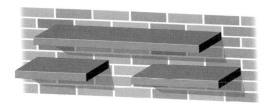

And the photo took on a life of its own. I eventually added to the backdrop: a globe, a plant, some books and figures of John F. Kennedy Jr. and Cookie Monster. But it was the photo that people wanted to talk about.

The tweets kept coming: mostly from Sox fans exulting in the happy memory, but others from bitter Yankees fans or, frankly, confused cable news viewers. I got asked about it on the street, and once, appropriately enough, at Fenway Park. I'm on *Morning Joe* most days and the show's host, Joe Scarborough, dubbed it "Perhaps the most meaningful historic photo since blurred images of troops landing on Normandy graced the cover of *Life* Magazine."

I heard from Varitek's wife, who said they were delighted. Viewers said they liked having a glimpse into my life and interests. The Athletic even wrote a piece about how I featured it in my shot. My answers about it—declaring it a defining American moment—always featured my tongue firmly planted in my cheek.

But it actually was silly and it was a distraction and it was about sports and the kind of stuff that we all cared about before the pandemic changed everything. It struck a chord. And if it prompted even a fleeting smile, it worked.

Plus, A-Rod had it coming.

— Jonathan Lemire

Setup Style #2

THE LIVING ROOM

You may choose the living room setup. Many of the top rooms we rate are living rooms. The chief advantage of the living room setup is depth. If you want depth—and why wouldn't you—the living room in most cases will offer the opportunity to showcase the most.

DANIEL GOLDMAN FORMER U.S. ATTORNEY, SOUTHERN DISTRICT OF NEW YORK

With opportunity come challenges. In particular, it will be crucial to keep in mind the lessons we will learn in the "Lighting" section later on. Your living room setup must be well lit from the foreground all the way to the back. In most or many cases, you will want to deploy lamps, sometimes several, in the foreground and the back of the space. In larger spaces, there may even be a lamp lighting up the middle of the space.

The living room setup is a showcase for many elements and features. It may in fact also use bookshelves or bookcases as a main if not the principal focus. It can be a great way to show that books are important to you, but that you also have a lot more to show. The living room will usually offer the best opportunity to showcase the art in your home (again, you'll want to check out our notes on lighting on page 225).

The key to the proper living room setup is its furniture and decorative items, like the all-important pillow. The couch you have is the couch you have. Except in the most egregious cases, we don't like to suggest wholesale changes, especially when they tend to be pricey. In all likelihood, the couch you have will present just fine. The not-so-secret key is pillows: how many and what they look like.

You will also have your chance to weigh in on the somewhat controversial karate chop pillow. That is, do you like pillows that have the "chopped" look at the top that gives rise to the term?

We are agnostic on the practice.

For effective teleconferencing purposes, you want bright pillows. Colors that pop. Choose colors with some contrast. Be free. Be expressive.

The pillow is the message. We have found that the pillow can be an effective way of making an important statement. Such a pillow can sometimes be called a branding pillow. We've seen great ones for NBC and the *Washington Post*. Those are fine for reporters and journalists, but most of us might look to

a pillow to say something as simple as "Love" or as meaning-ful as Connie Schultz's First Amendment pillow. And we may be biased, but we certainly appreciated Michigan governor Gretchen Whitmer's surprise showing of the Room Rater pillow.

Pillows don't only go on couches, of course. The single chair/pillow combo is a timeless classic.

Not everyone will end up with an actual Eames chair—indeed, not all will aspire to. But if you decide this midcentury classic is a must, you may want to consider a high-quality reproduction, as an original from Herman Miller starts at about $6,999.

Nearly any living room chair will benefit from the addition of a pillow. Attractive pillows or pillow covers are quite affordable, can add that all-important pop of color, and can say

something about you as well. Ignore the pillow at your own peril.

Adding flowers or plants, or both, will improve most living room set-ups. (See "Plants vs. Succulents" and "Flowers.") In most cases, if you choose flowers you will want to place them in the near foreground on an end table/side table or available counter or shelf. In some cases, having a lovely bouquet in the middle of the living room, often on the coffee table, can work well. Generally speaking, flowers will not work well at the end of the living room, whereas plants, depending on the variety, can work throughout.

The living room may be the best opportunity to showcase the art you favor. (See "Art Styles.") The key, as is often the case, is to make sure the art you select is well lit. Whether it's an original oil painting, a movie poster, or other wall art, we strongly recommend having it framed. While we don't care how much you paid for your art, we do feel you can go a long way simply by framing what you have. There are very few times when having unframed wall art is acceptable. One case where framing is not expected or desired is with textiles.

COUCH VS. SOFA

There was a time when it mattered, but that time has passed. Sure. It may matter to the design maven in your life when you say couch and they say "It's a sofa." It matters to few others, and at this point, if you use the terms interchangeably you're on pretty comfortable ground either way.

If you want to maintain the illusion that it matters, you can learn that *couch* comes from the French *coucher,* meaning "to lie down." You may want to consider that *sofa* comes from the Arabic *ṣuffah,* referring to a bench covered with pillows and blankets. Whatever.

If you want to deal with the terms somewhat more practically, you can consider that a sofa usually refers to a larger, more formal piece with sitting room for more people. The couch is usually smaller and may be thought of as more casual.

Does it matter? No. It does not.

The Couch View

Beware the couch view.

It seems as though a solid 20 percent of video calls are positioned with the subject seated on their couch. It seems natural. They have a couch. They may even have art above it and maybe a lamp next to it. Why not set up the camera/device in front of it? They can, and many do.

This is what we call the couch view.

But results are mixed at best, and in all likelihood, you'll be positioned too low. Couches are meant to be low, which is great for relaxing, reading, or enjoying a movie. Visually, with proper pillow placement, they can be quite appealing. The issue is that when you are Zooming, you don't want to be seated low— you want to be upright. Furthermore, your art, when hung at a normal height, will often appear far too high if you are seated on the couch.

But do not worry, because there is a better way: Take a basic dining room chair. Position it in front of the couch and set up there. It's the best of both worlds. Make the couch and art above it part of the setup. Crop your shot so we see the art—not just the bottom edge as will often be the case.

PILLOWS VS. CUSHIONS

Technically, there really is a difference between pillows and cushions. Although most people now use the two words interchangeably, pillows are on beds and cushions are on couches and chairs, outside the bedroom. Or put more simply, pillows are for your head and cushions are for décor.

The first known use of the word *pillow* was in the twelfth century. Historically, pillows were made with natural materials and used to support the head and body while sleeping. Today, they can be decorative as well as supportive and are made with man-made materials, but their main purpose remains functional.

Cushions, on the other hand, are mentioned early in the Middle Ages in the houses of wealthy people. Today, they are mainly accent pieces and add texture and color to furnishings. In fact, they are often considered upholstery in and of themselves.

Pillow Talk

LATOSHA BROWN ACTIVIST

Yes, pillows talk—they tell you a lot about a home. Pillows are the language of one's home décor style. The presence of a simple set of pillows can transform the entire landscape and feel of a room, camouflage the age of existing furniture, and communicate the purpose or use of a space.

Adding a few bright-colored or modern-styled pillows will take a room a quantum leap into the future. Great Art Deco pillows will immediately modernize your existing living room furniture, making it look years younger. Placing a simple set of boldly colored decorative pillows will transform the entire color palette of your space and can be an essential tie-in for every element of a room.

While pillows are strong visual communicators, they also serve the purpose of expanding the utility and function of a room. Oversized pillows can instantly turn a floor into a welcoming sitting area for family and friends. Pillows strategically placed in a corner or window seat can be a subtle invitation for family and visitors to take a seat and/or experience a new view in an underutilized or uncommon space.

Whenever I select pillows for my home, I keep three goals in mind:

1. to create a welcoming space
2. to communicate the theme and purpose of my room
3. to add a little of my personality to the space

In my home I have a very clear vision of how I want each of my spaces to be utilized. I have a formal room, a family room, a TV room, a dining room, a workspace room, a playroom, and of course my favorite—my bedroom! I use pillows to help set the tone and the temperature for each room. In each room I start with the pillows in mind. The entire room décor is anchored by whatever pillows I select.

Therefore, each year I plan the great pillow shopping day with my niece to scour the city for interesting pillows so I can "redecorate" my home in a way that aligns it with my theme for the new season.

On our pillow shopping trips we rate pillows by quality of fabric, pattern, color, shape, size, and utility. Then of course there are seasonal choices for holidays, birthdays, and other special events and family moments.

After a tumultuous 2020 election year, I needed to bring energy into my home that communicated calmness, stability, and safety—so I changed all my pillows to pastel and neutral tones. After a year of being inundated and dealing with COVID-19, a divisive political environment, voter suppression, racial tension on the national level, and an intense campaign season, all I needed to be reminded of whenever I walked through my home was the beauty of simplicity, safety, and silence. There was enough happening in the social and political arena that I just needed something simple and safe.

What are you communicating with your pillow choices? If *your* pillows could talk, what would you really want them to say?

—Latosha Brown

KIMBERLY ATKINS STOHR | COLUMNIST, *THE BOSTON GLOBE*

Don't be afraid of color—it really pops on-screen and is a way to show a bit of your personality. Fresh flowers are great, but invest in a set of really good artificial ones as well to use in a pinch. And everyone loves a pet—but they are better depicted in a picture than in the furry flesh. You don't want to be upstaged.

—Kimberly Atkins Stohr

ROOM RATER TOP NO-NOs

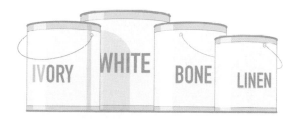

No-No #2: Monochromatic

Monochromatic. We say this with regret. Monochromatic design is what you have when multiple nuanced shades of one basic color are spread across a room, covering every surface from drapes to walls to furniture to flooring. If done well, it can be gorgeous. If not, it can look like a Stanley Kubrick set.

The issue is that monochromatic designs tend to look especially off on video. If you have a well-done monochromatic setup, at least add a proverbial splash of color or three.

Beams

Who doesn't love an exposed beam? They have gained popularity in recent decades, as industrial and rustic home designs have become common and desired. Exposed beams are a feature in architecture that enables your room to have higher ceilings. During the 1970s, there was a back-to-nature movement and beams gained new fans. But beams have been around since ancient times and have proven their longevity, style, and durability.

The type of construction known as post and beam is the result of a process called timber framing, which has been around since ancient Egypt in 2000 BC. It was used through the centuries all over Europe and then made its way to North America. The technique was employed by the first settlers and was later combined with brick for house construction.

The rustic and natural elements of our architectural history appeal to many of us trying to connect to our past. Whether your beams are left alone or painted, this trend isn't going away.

Home Office

One development of the last few years has been the increased importance of having a comfortable home office space. And let's face it, for many of us, our "home office" is also a guest room, a gym, or a spare TV room. Working from home is now more common and less of an exception, and many companies are shifting to a hybrid model of home/office for the long haul. So take down the clothes you have drying on that elliptical, dust off the old printer you no longer use, and let's get started.

Just as you don't want rarely used gym equipment or outdated office machines to be dominant features people see in your home office Zoom calls, you also don't want the place to look like a sparse cubicle. Before you turn your "home gym" into an office, decide exactly what you need to do your job, and then build around that.

One of the best ways to reduce clutter and make your home office look larger is to get things off the floor and surfaces, just as with any other small space. Invest in some floating shelves and organizational items, as these will look better and be helpful to your workday. Vertical file folders on the desk will look neat, and invest in storage containers or baskets to keep paper in. Most people forget that wall space can be used to organize, and it will look cleaner.

Office equipment and technology aren't pretty. We see most of our dreaded cord violations in offices (see "Violation #1: The Cord Violation"). Make sure you place your equipment as close to electrical outlets as possible. Invest in fabric cord covers, winders, tubing, or a wire organizer. Once the unsightly cords are out of the way, your space will be tidy and clean for video calls.

A chair may be your most important investment because of the time you will be spending in it. A good one does not have to be ugly. The desk, of course, is another major item—spending the time and money to find one that works for you and will last is vital.

We still see a lot of beige walls in home offices, but we have noticed more of an effort to spice up otherwise drab and boring spaces. A bright, cheery color on the walls might be just the thing to make your work life happier.

When possible, set up your chair and desk so you can look out a window. It will do wonders for your workday, and natural light is always preferred over artificial lighting. However, if you do not have windows, facing a nice photo or piece of art can do the trick.

Personalizing your home office will soften a hard institutional look. Photos, art (especially kids' art), and office supplies that are bright will make the room warm and inviting, and a place you  want to spend time in. Pick things that will inspire you or bring to mind a treasured memory. Mouse pads, coffee mugs, and the like can add a bit of color and energy to any environment.

ROOM RATER TOP TIPS

PETER BAKER AND SUSAN GLASSER POLITICAL JOURNALISTS, AUTHORS

We're print people, so the idea of setting up live shots from our home was a little out of our comfort zone. There are so many factors to take into consideration that baffle the print mind—lighting, backdrop, ambient sounds, angle, framing, Wi-Fi location, and, not inconsiderable, our dog, Ellie, who has wandered her way onto television more than once. We got a lot of good tips from Room Rater's evaluations of our appearances and those of others. And we have learned how hard our television colleagues work to make their programs so professional.

For us, there is the extra challenge of being a two-network household, Susan on CNN and Peter on MSNBC. On some occasions, we have had hits scheduled at the exact same time, in which case we have to decide who will sit where. Usually, one of us takes the living room while the other takes the kitchen. We have to make sure to shut doors that usually stay open between them to keep the noise of one of our shots from being heard in the other. We have to bribe the dog with treats to sit quietly on the couch. And we have to pray that the Wi-Fi can handle two video calls simultaneously—there have been times when it was overloaded and one or both of us lost connections.

On occasion, we appear together, usually not on television but for book talks, panel discussions, college lectures, or other appearances. In those cases, we've concluded that it works better to sit next to each other in the same shot rather than have each of us on separate laptops in separate rooms appearing in separate boxes on the screen. It makes it easier to have a conversation that way. And we enjoy being side by side more anyway. It's not quite date night, but we're lucky to get to work together.

—Peter Baker and Susan Glasser

Maps Are Art

How Cartography
Can Be Your Friend

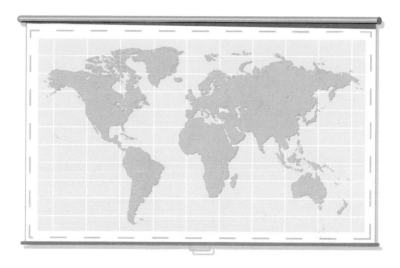

Maps are not only informative and instructional but can be pleasing aesthetically as well. Many exceptional rooms rely on maps as décor/art, but maps also help tell your viewer something about you. Maybe you chose a map of the state you're from. Maybe you selected a map that honors your ancestry.

Many people find that antique maps, or at least antique-looking maps, are the way to go. Others prefer something a little more up-to-date. As with other art, maps should generally be framed. We look askance at anything art-related taped to the wall (with the notable exception of kids' art).

In some instances, a large framed map can be the focal point of a wall, to great effect.

(For the purposes of this book, globes as decorative objects are considered separately from maps.)

CONNIE SCHULTZ COLUMNIST, *USA TODAY*

In the beginning of pandemic TV, as I've come to think of it, audience critics weighed in with suggestions. All of my interviews take place at my desk in my home office, and some didn't like the clutter of my background: too many books, too many family photos, too many blah-blah-blah. I made few changes, as this is where I write and teach, and I didn't see any point in pretending otherwise. I did add a small console table behind me, which I used to display a vintage brass pineapple and a rotating arrangement of house plants and flowers.

(cont.)

Over time, audience members seemed to be more forgiving. They started mentioning how "authentic" my setup looked, how "normal" I seemed to be. Viewers had their favorite things. Lots of comments about the First Amendment pillow, which for years has rested in my rocking chair in the corner, and the framed Beatles photo, a gift from my father when I was in first grade. I started fielding more questions about my jewelry—most of it made by female artists—and words of encouragement about my increasingly long hair, which became a kaleidoscope of missteps with do-it-yourself dyes. (Note: "warm" means red.) These generous comments would have delighted my working-class mother, gone twenty-two years now. In her view, I would forever represent the people I come from, and should aspire to bring the best version of myself, without pretense. Sound advice for pandemic TV. For life too.

—Connie Schultz

PLANTS VS. SUCCULENTS

A quick note about choosing which plants are best for your space, particularly in regard to creating great Zoom rooms.

All succulents are plants, but not all plants are succulents. Because of their fleshy stems, roots, and leaves, succulents retain water, so those of you who forget to water will have much better luck with succulents. Cacti are the most famous group in this botanical family, but there are so many more choices. In recent years, succulents have become trendy in home design, perhaps because of the low-maintenance aspect, but also because many people live in smaller dwellings like condos and apartments than ever before, and it just makes more sense to have smaller plants in your space. Another reason for the growing popularity of succulents is that they come in a variety of bright colors and interesting shapes.

FERN

SPIDER

IVY

SEMPERVIVUM

ALOE VERA

PALM

Best Houseplants–
How to Achieve a Strong Plant Game

The strongest plant games we have seen in Zoom rooms are usually a combination of traditional house plants and succulents. The ideal types and sizes of multiple foliage in your room will depend on the room size and composition. Bright pots and vases also add color and texture and sometimes depth to any room. Here are some of our favorite and most commonly seen plants:

1. Ivy (especially in an indoor basket)
2. Aloe vera
3. Palm
4. Hens and chicks (Sempervivum)
5. Spider plant
6. Fern

Succulent Care

In any event, there are many choices if you choose to green up your room with succulents rather than more traditional choices. As they can get infections from overwatering, the best and simplest rule of thumb for all species is to leave them alone with adequate sunlight. Waiting until the soil is completely dried out before watering them is your best bet. That is usually one week or so, depending on other factors like humidity, temperature, and drainage. If the leaves start stretching, they are not getting enough sunlight. Another important tip for successful succulents is the potting mix and container factor. Both must drain well. One suggestion is to fill the bottom of your container with small rocks so that the water drains away from the roots.

Some of our favorites are aloe vera, jade, snake plant (Sansevieria), zebra plant, hens and chicks (Sempervivum), various Echeveria, cacti, and several types of Dracaena.

Flowers

PHILIP RUCKER   SENIOR WASHINGTON CORRESPONDENT,
THE WASHINGTON POST

Most people can keep a plant alive, and if they can't, faux plants will suffice. Fresh flowers, however, take much work, but they are worth the extra time and effort. At the very least, find some that look real enough to pass the Zoom call test. They add that spot of color, complement décor, and make you look like you care.

You can choose your favorite blooms or the most fragrant, but here are a few of the most popular we've seen and the ones we enjoy looking at the most.

HYDRANGEAS The name comes from the Greek words *hydor,* which means "water," and *angeion,* which means "vessel," because they resemble water jugs. Hydrangeas come in many vibrant colors, like purple, pink, blue, and green, and also pastels and white.

TULIPS Always a favorite, tulips were first cultivated by the Ottomans and exported to Holland, where they were perfected. They are available in every color imaginable.

LILIES Lilies were big in mythology and the Bible. (Remember Easter lilies?) They are colorful and visually stunning because the flowers are large. They also come in a variety of shapes and sizes.

ROSES   Roses are never going away. The fossil record dates the rose as about 35 million years old. China began cultivation five thousand years ago, and roses have been the go-to flower since then.

DAFFODILS   Daffodils have been a garden favorite since around 300 BC. They were brought to Britain by the Romans and have been popular ever since. The flowers are shaped like a trumpet and come in the traditional bright yellow and some other hues.

BLACK-EYED SUSANS   This flower has many species and is native to the prairies of North America. The brilliant yellow brightens any space, and there are other shades equally vibrant, making them a favorite in home décor.

ROOM RATER TOP TIPS

ROBERT GIBBS FORMER WHITE HOUSE PRESS SECRETARY

Own and personalize your space. Flowers, to me, are key as they're easy to add and change (unlike, say, tile). Something fresh and colorful is pleasant to the viewer's eye and easily noticed. Change your fruit up, too. Keen watchers will call you out if it looks like your apples haven't moved in weeks. Balance your digital picture with these, so people see the pleasing edges and can focus on you in the middle.

—Robert Gibbs

VALERIE JARRETT FORMER OBAMA SENIOR ADVISER

White Phalaenopsis orchids brighten any room. There's no such thing as too many orchids. Thankfully, it is nearly impossible to kill them if you put them in indirect light and give them two to four ice cubes a week. They last for months...and then about six months later they bloom again.

—Valerie Jarrett

ZAIN VELJI   PARTNER, NORTHWEATHER

Knitted Succulents

They say not all heroes wear capes: Some wear yarn. Well, if they don't wear yarn, they bring a yarn succulent to your door.

Confused? You should be. You see, my Room Rater ratings consisted of scores well below a 10/10—a shameful 7, an embarrassing 8, a quasi-respectful 9, but never a 10. I lobbied. I pleaded. I launched a campaign. But the 10 remained elusive. Feedback was unanimous: I lacked a succulent.

Turn to my hero (he made me write this part), Mayor Naheed Nenshi, then-mayor of Calgary. The purple crusader himself, bringing me a late-afternoon delivery, just in time for a political pundit hit on the state broadcaster. Skeptical of my horticultural prowess, His Worship procured a tiny cactus made of yarn. All my other plants are dead, but this lovingly stitched succulent prevailed. I was finally awarded my perfect score.

—Zain Velji

Keeping It Real
FAKE PLANTS

It helps if you think of them as silk flowers, as many of the better artificial flowers are. It also helps if you're not a purist and are willing to accept compromise.

We'd love it if every bouquet were real and grown in a greenhouse. It would be great if every tall fig plant were purchased young and nurtured by you into maturity. And in many cases they are. But we do not sit in judgment of specific decisions made where practicality rules the day.

If you want to stop by the florist or the supermarket floral section and pick up a weekly arrangement, then bless you. If you have the skills and energy to grow and maintain house plants, that's great. That said, we don't begrudge the choices you make.

A Few of Our Favorite Things
Knitted Succulents

Some people can't keep real plants alive, and for those people, there are alternatives. One of our very favorites is the knitted succulent.

Presidential
ROOM RATER

MICHAEL BESCHLOSS — PRESIDENTIAL HISTORIAN

FDR

Franklin D. Roosevelt once told Orson Welles that they were the "two greatest actors in the United States." He knew that an actor required a stage. When he took power in 1933, the president's offices in the West Wing (built by Theodore Roosevelt in 1902) were modest and rarely photographed. The following year, FDR had that edifice gutted and rebuilt, with a new, much big-

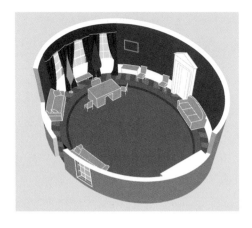
ger and oval (mimicking the shape of the Blue Room in the White House residence) office on the corner, overlooking the Rose Garden and the South Grounds. Many people mistakenly presume that this chamber dates back somehow to Washington or Jefferson, but it is actually less than a century old. By Roosevelt's order (he was an amateur architect who made rough sketches for federal post offices and Bethesda Naval Hospital, now Walter Reed), tall French windows were built to drench the room with sunlight. Most of the woodwork and plasterwork are an early 1930s World's Fair Art Deco version of Federal design, with built-in half-shell bookcases and overly bold cornices. Atop FDR's desk (inherited from his predecessor, Herbert Hoover, whom he had defeated and then banned from the White House for the twelve years of his presidency), were a telephone with no dial; tiny photos of his four sons, who all fought in World War II; an early digital clock; and little gimcracks from a life-

time in politics. Unable to walk without assistance, Roosevelt almost always greeted visitors while sitting down behind his desk and was often photographed that way—so his setting was important. He enhanced the grandeur of the presidency (FDR was easily the most powerful chief executive up to then) by creating the most extravagant American presidential office in history, and—but for changes in flooring, wall color, curtains, lighting, accessories, and furniture—Roosevelt's self-invented stage-set-in-the-round is the same one presidents use today.

JFK

Unlike FDR, Harry Truman, and Dwight Eisenhower, who had visitors sit on hard chairs for a presidential audience in front of their desk, Jacqueline Kennedy thought the oval chamber should be outfitted more like "a New England sitting room." For the first time, she had facing sofas and a coffee table placed in front of the old fireplace, allowing JFK to chat with visitors while rocking in the Carolina chair his doctor, Janet Travell, had prescribed to ease his injured back. The new First Lady discovered, on the White House ground floor, a desk, covered in green baize, that had been an 1880 gift of the British government;

it was constructed from oaken timbers taken from the once-abandoned RMS *Resolute,* which the United States had sailed back to London. FDR had installed a door on the kneehole of the desk, emblazoned with the presidential seal, to conceal his leg braces. Young Caroline and John Kennedy and their cousins and friends loved to climb under the desk and pop the door open, surprising presidential guests. (The now-famous Resolute desk has been used by every president since Kennedy, save Johnson, Nixon, Ford, and George H. W. Bush.) On his desktop, JFK displayed the mounted coconut he had heroically used to send his SOS when his *PT-109* sank in the South Pacific in World War II, a green crocodile desk set given him by Charles de Gaulle, and two pieces of his beloved scrimshaw. On the walls were dramatic paintings of naval war scenes, as well as depictions of Native Americans by George Catlin and a photograph of a sailboat. Behind Kennedy's desk, over his shoulders, were two lantern sconces recalling revolutionary Boston and Paul Revere. Kennedy gave most of his major addresses (Berlin Crisis 1961, Cuban Missile Crisis 1962, civil rights 1963) from behind the Resolute desk, but in that age, presidential TV was almost always in black-and-white. Viewers saw little of JFK's office; before speeches, a neutral TV background panel was set up behind the president's chair. When Kennedy flew to Texas in November 1963, his Oval Office was being transformed, at Jackie's behest (counseled by her Paris designer, Stéphane Boudin), in a way that would have suited the era of color television. The old pale green walls were painted white; the heavy green curtains that dated back to FDR were replaced by more open, long, straight white ones to let in more sunlight, and the old green oval rug gave way to a new oval one that was fire-engine red. Workmen were completing Jackie's Oval Office makeover at the moment when, thousands of miles away, shots were fired at the president's motorcade in Dallas. Three days after the assassination, the new president, Lyndon Johnson, moved into Kennedy's office. LBJ had ridden in the fatal motorcade, and when he saw the new, very red rug, he was shaken, for it made him think of his predecessor's blood. Soon it was banished from the room.

Ronald Reagan

Ronald and Nancy Reagan, the first professional actors to serve as president and First Lady, did not need to be tutored to know that the Oval Office was a stage. Asked if he planned to work in a smaller hideaway office, as Nixon and Jimmy Carter had, Reagan shook his head and said he had spent too much time and effort trying to get into the big oval one to do that. Entering the presidency amid a deep recession, he tried to signal frugality by keeping the orange-and-gold Ford-Carter rug and curtains, which coincidentally echoed some of the sunset colors of the Reagan Ranch in California's San Jacinto Mountains. When he delivered his first Oval Office speech on the economy, visible on the table behind him were a photograph of Reagan and his daughter, Patti, embracing in that room, and a photo of a smiling Nancy with her arms crossed. In 1980, the Reagan campaign had used TV commercials that were almost deliberately unpolished, so the candidate would not look too Hollywood slick. In this first speech from the Resolute desk, the sixty-nine-year-old president was so amateurishly lit and made up that he looked older than his age. Throughout his two terms, Reagan kept plaques on his desktop saying IT CAN BE DONE and THE BUCKAROO STOPS HERE, as well as a space-age gold clock and glass souvenirs that would have seemed at home atop the Denver oil mogul Blake Carrington's desk on ABC's much-viewed evening soap opera of that time,

Dynasty. (Blake would have liked Reagan's potted palms too.) Anyone who doubted that Reagan saw the Oval Office as a studio should have been present on his last morning in office in January 1989. With a photographer snapping away, in carefully staged scenes that resembled the frame-by-frame  sketches employed by Alfred Hitchcock in his filmmaking, the outgoing president was shown, as his archives tell us, "talking on the telephone" and "leaving the Oval Office for the last time" and then "walking along the White House colonnade and waving goodbye." Long before his presidency, Reagan had been speaking directly to the camera, attracting large audiences, on *General Electric Theater* and *Death Valley Days.* As a genuine actor—in contrast with FDR, who thought of himself as one, or JFK, who liked to spend time with Hollywood celebrities—Reagan knew that this skill, which brought him two presidential landslides and helped him weather the Iran-Contra scandal, did not depend very much on how that Oval Office looked.

—Michael Beschloss

Alternative Setup

STYLE #1

THE PORCH

This category also can include the outdoor living space (OLS).

Porches are rooms. Sort of. Either way, they are part of many video calls. How's your Wi-Fi? If it is solid, setting up on the porch can be a workable option. Porch furniture can work nicely. Especially if yours includes a decorative pillow or two.

If the time of day is right, this is a great way to celebrate your use of natural light. That being said, there's no rule against throwing a ring light into the mix.

As with other setups, details matter. The porch setup is a great place for hanging plants, and they will help frame your background. We like wind chimes, but their use on a windy day may be problematic. On the other hand, a gentle tinkling may work well on all but the breeziest days. If the weather is truly bad you are best staying off the porch anyway.

Of course, the porch does come with its own share of risks and challenges. There is a degree of unpredictability here in that you will be more exposed to whatever noises your neighbors decide to inflict upon you. You never know when Bob from across the street is going to fire up the lawn mower or leaf blower for some spontaneous landscaping.

WICKER OR RATTAN?

SEN. ELIZABETH WARREN (D) MASSACHUSETTS

While these terms are often used interchangeably, they are not the same. Rattan is the material that wicker is often made from.

Wicker is a style of weaving furniture that has existed for millennia. It dates back to ancient Egypt—in fact, archeologists have found wicker furniture thousands of years old, including inside tombs of the pharaohs. More recently, wicker saw a rebirth in popularity as part of the Arts and Crafts movement beginning in the early twentieth century.

Rattan is a material related to bamboo that is often used in wicker-style furnishings. Rattan, part of the bamboo family, is native to parts of Asia, Africa, and Australia. Its weight, flexibility, and durability make it a good material for weaving furniture using the wicker technique.

ROOM RATER TOP TIPS

MONICA LEWINSKY AUTHOR/ACTIVIST

Here's what I love about Room Rater: it makes me think of my late grandma. She had the best decorative eye and would have loved something like this. (If she'd understood the internet...she was in her eighties in the late nineties.)

—Monica Lewinsky

Violation #1

THE CORD VIOLATION

What are cord violations? Why are they objectionable? What do we do about them?

We all have our pet peeves. Welcome to ours. Behold, the cord violation.

To be sure, some cord violations in some settings are more easily forgiven than others, and we try to be sensitive to that. For example, musicians in studios are normally exempt from cord violations. However, if you place the same musician in their living room or kitchen with an obvious cord, they will be pinged too.

But what exactly is a cord violation? A cord violation is almost any visible electrical cord, phone charging cord, or wire trailing out from a socket that is visible in your Zoom shot.

With just a little planning and forethought, cord violations are some of the easier Room Rater faux pas to avoid. Kitchen shot? Have a cord showing? If you're not going to be using the coffeepot during your Zoom call or TV hit, just unplug the cord and hide it behind the pot. That's it. Simple, right? In other cases, you'll want to use some form of camouflage. Try moving the spice jars. Or reposition the fruit bowl. We have found that a well-positioned floor plant can do wonders not just for bringing color to a room but for hiding unsightly cords.

Here are some ground rules on cords. If you have a cord in view that is not providing light or otherwise in use, you are probably better off to "unplug and tuck." If the cord in view is attached to a lamp, you'll want to turn the lamp so that the cord is away from the camera, hopefully with the body of the lamp obscuring most or all of the cord.

A lot of cord violations can be avoided with a slight adjustment in composition. Set up your shot. Look at it. If you have lamps or other appliances plugged into a visible socket, you may be best tightening the shot slightly or panning left or right.

Solutions for the Chronic Cord Violator: Cord and Cable Management Tips

There are a number of cord organizers on the market that can save you from the headaches of last-minute cord untangling. Some of our favorites include cable zippers, cable boxes, cable clips, and hanging cable organizers. We recommend browsing among these options and picking the one that works for you depending on the look you are going for and the number of cables you are dealing with.

The Animals
OF ROOM RATER

FLUFFY ROOMS

As mentioned earlier, some of our best photobombs are when the pets drop in for a visit during a meeting. Sometimes it's barking, or a quick run-by, or doing something naughty/destructive/distracting in the background. We love animals, so when they show up in a shot doing something our own pets would do, like eating, sleeping, or trying to get our attention, those of us who cohabitate with animals can relate.

By far the most common animal activity in the Skype rooms we see is sleeping: on the couch, on the chair, on the floor, on the windowsill, on the patio, or on the bed. There is something calming about that, and it softens any space. Pets can break the ice on TV as well as in meetings. They're an easy subject of discussion, because everyone loves to talk about their animal roommates. There's a reason social media is full of cute animal photos, videos, and accounts. They give us a break from the ugly stuff. Our advice is very easy on this subject: animals are welcome.

In fact, some animals had rooms so fabulous they somehow managed to send us photos of their habitats. (We suspect their humans may have helped, but we can't be sure.) There were dogs, cats, rabbits, lizards, and birds. Our special animal correspondent, Lorenzo the Cat, will be taking a look at some of our best fluffy rooms and how animals improve any space they are in.

Guest Column by Lorenzo the Cat

Lorenzo's Bio

A Maine Coon with the patience of a Buddhist monk and the soul of a philosopher, Lorenzo the Cat was tossed in a garbage can and left for dead on the day he was born. Today he is a professional model who happens to like wearing clothes, preferably those with a casual tropical flair.

Photos of him have been exhibited in museums and galleries across the US, and he's even "hanging" in the permanent collection of the Feline Historical Museum in Alliance, Ohio.

His home base is Miami, where he enjoys taking naps in the sun, chasing lizards, and watching the wild peacocks that strut through his neighborhood. He's popular on social media and can occasionally be highly opinionated, especially when it comes to animal rights.

Lorenzo lives with photographer/writer Joann Biondi, who uses him as her artistic muse. He thinks she gets far more credit than she deserves, because he's the one who really does all the work.

Levi

My friend Levi is one lucky dog. For the first two years of his life, he was chained, beaten, and almost starved to death in a West Virginia compound. But then he was rescued and his life was transformed.

He is now the Pennsylvania State Dog and lives with Lieutenant Governor John Fetterman, his wife, Gisele, and their three children. Levi is a mixed-breed with a warm golden coat and big soulful eyes. When he was first adopted by the Fettermans at the start of the COVID pandemic, he weighed only thirty-five pounds. He had fleas, worms, and Lyme disease. He was skittish and so frightened that he fell asleep standing up and then had nightmares.

All of that is gone now, and today he's a sturdy seventy-five-pound love machine who demands belly rubs, likes playing tug-of-war with his toys, and begs to go for rides in a pickup truck. He loves to eat chicken, cheese, and the occasional shoe. He works tirelessly at raising people's awareness of other animals in need and is also an advocate for the downtrodden and marginalized members of the human species. Levi is very popular on social media, and he has friends in high places.

He lives in an industrial-chic loft adorned with a vintage American flag and lots of cool antiques in the Braddock suburb of Pittsburgh. His photogenic face is always a treat to behold. Whether he's spotted in the background of a TV news segment wagging his tail or making an accidental appearance in a Zoom meeting, Levi's presence has a calming effect on all who see him.

He is also a perfect example of what a little bit of love, patience, and generosity can do for any living creature.

Coava

Nobody can resist a bunny butt. Plopped on a computer keyboard, sprawled out on a hardwood floor, or perched on a sleek office chair, a cute bunny butt always makes for the best photobomb. Weighing in at about six pounds, my friend Coava adds a rich, velvety softness to every Zoom room he appears in.

A domestic breed known as a Mini Rex, Coava has a plush, dark gray coat and long white whiskers that twitch when he's curious. His ears, almost always upright, have a pretty pink tint on the inside. His little button nose just naturally grabs attention.

Coava was adopted from a Los Angeles County animal shelter in March 2020 and has since lived happily ever after with podcast host Kenny Holmes and his wife, Elva. They live in a contemporary Los Angeles home with a neutral palette of tans, browns, and blacks that are perfectly coordinated with the bunny's natural coloring. Coava is even better than a carefully chosen accent pillow.

Although he is not supposed to climb up the spiral staircase in the living room, he occasionally can't resist the temptation and breaks the rules. He will also come racing around a corner if his treat jar is shaken, and then look up with those keen black eyes that say, "Treats, please."

While not as common as cats and dogs, rabbits can indeed make excellent animal companions and are wonderful teachers of compassion for children. They make very little noise, can be litter box–trained as Coava has been, and are relatively low-maintenance. They're surprisingly intelligent as well as lively and affectionate. And because they're unconventional, they demonstrate that it's okay to be a little bit different with your lifestyle choices.

Carla

People often boast that they rescued an animal, but sometimes it's the other way around. Especially in the case of my friend Carla Tortelli Nichols.

A fluffy black mixed-breed feline with intense green eyes and a white puff on her chest, Carla literally saved her humans' lives.

One cold December night in 2017, while author Tom Nichols

and his wife, Lynn, were sound asleep, Carla jumped on their bed, crawled on top of them, and started pounding them on their heads to wake them up. She was relentless.

The family's smoke alarm had not kicked in yet, but Carla smelled smoke and instinctively knew that danger was in the air. It's called animal intelligence. Soon after, a raging fire tore through the second floor of the Nicholses' Rhode Island home. Fortunately, everyone escaped unharmed. Thanks to Carla, of course.

She has never let the family forget her act of heroism. These days, Carla is the real star of the household and pretty much gets whatever she wants, including the occasional hunk of rare filet mignon. She's also a highly skilled mouser who proudly carries her live prey in her mouth in anticipation of lavish praise. Weighing in at a slim and girlish nine pounds, she is in fact about twelve years old. Carla has come a long way from when she was abandoned on the streets of Newport, taken in by a kind veterinary clinic, and then adopted by Tom.

Whether she's sitting beside a desktop computer, lounging on a living room sofa, or playing with catnip toys on an old Persian rug, when Carla makes an appearance during a Zoom call or photobombs a television interview, all is well with the world.

Setup Style #3
THE KITCHEN

When Room Rater began in the early days of the pandemic, we had no idea the kitchen setup would become one of the best background alternatives for those looking to break free from the Bookcase Industrial Complex.

Without a doubt, the kitchen setup has established itself as a mainstay and is here for good.

JOHN HEILEMANN NATIONAL AFFAIRS ANALYST/NBC, MSNBC

There are two basic approaches to using your kitchen as a background. The first is to show one wall of the kitchen, typically with cabinets above and/or wall-hugging counter below. The camera or laptop can be set up on an opposite counter or on an island. As is frequently the case, choosing the right number of books to bring the shot to eye level is essential. Like the basic book setup, this is the easiest to pull off. As with the books, you will want to work with/adjust your spacing to create the most flattering depth.

STEVE SCHMIDT — AMERICAN POLITICAL STRATEGIST

The second approach can be thought of as the whole-kitchen shot. It can be shot at an angle, which works best for larger kitchens with an island. In general, if you can work the island into the shot, that is best. For narrower galley-style kitchens, you'll normally want to set up your camera/device to shoot straight down the kitchen, maximizing depth.

As with other setup options, the key to a well-presented kitchen setup is in the details. A nicely arranged assortment of spices can make all the difference, for example. If your kitchen has good tile work—especially a backsplash— make sure it's well lit and not overly obscured.

It's completely acceptable for a reasonable number of small appliances to be within view. In fact, it's an opportunity to add a splash of color and design sense. A nice coffeemaker can add a lot. As can a nice blender. We'd recommend putting some thought into the shape of your toaster. A retro-style four-slicer can be a bonus. We are pro–toaster oven.

It's important when setting up your kitchen shot not to make it look barren or sterile. People want to visualize you cooking at that stove. Chopping vegetables on those countertops. To that end, show us the hanging cutting board, the knife block. There is a fine line, however. People want to see a kitchen that is in use, but not one that is untidy. No dirty dishes should be in the sink.

We like to see hanging pots and spice racks. There are some things we don't recommend having within view. We have environmental concerns with K-Cup displays. We suggest putting them out of sight.

On the stove is a good place to add the proverbial splash of color with an appropriately colored teakettle. If you're lucky enough to have one, a classic Le Creuset cast-iron red-orange pot on the stove adds color and sends a message of culinary sophistication.

As with other setups, most will be improved by flowers or plants. In particular, we like to see fresh flowers placed on the counter or island. It adds another note of color and freshness.

The risk of cord violations (see "Violation #1: The Cord Violation") is higher in the kitchen than in any other setup. You'll want to take special care that the cords for the appliances are blocked or carefully unplugged and tucked out of view.

Lighting is always critical. If you have under-cabinet lights, in most cases you'll want them turned on.

Claire's Recipes

FMR. SEN. CLAIRE MCCASKILL (D) MISSOURI

Okay, guys, here goes. As my grandmother taught me, it is always okay to steal someone else's recipe. She died owning hundreds of cookbooks. She read them like novels. And she used many of the recipes from those books for family and church occasions. She adjusted recipes she used to make them better, but I never recall her saying that something was "from the *Joy of Cooking* cookbook with a few tweaks." I just remember everyone saying, "Did you try Mildred's chocolate cake?" So to call anything "my recipe" is dangerous. I will try to give credit to the main source of the recipes below.

Fresh Strawberry Layer Cake

Adapted from MyRecipes.com

Preheat the oven to 350 degrees.

Grease and flour two 9" round pans.

Whisk together 3 cups cake flour with 1 tablespoon baking powder and a pinch of salt. Set aside.

Beat a cup of salted butter at room temperature until fluffy and then slowly add 2 cups granulated sugar. Next add 4 egg yolks, one at a time.

Alternate adding the flour mixture and 1 cup of milk. Add 2 teaspoons of vanilla extract at the end.

Then beat the 4 egg whites at high speed until stiff and then fold one-third of them in at a time. Place batter in the two pans and bake until the toothpick comes out clean. In my oven they take about 25 minutes. Start checking them then.

Cool them down for a little bit before turning them out.

Time to make the icing:
Stir together ¼ cup granulated sugar and 8 ounces of mascarpone cheese. Set aside.

Whip 2 cups of whipping cream until stiff, slowly adding in another ⅓ cup of granulated sugar.

Fold the cheese mixture into the whipped cream in 3 batches.

Take fresh strawberries and slice a thin layer off the stem end so they will sit flat.

Back to the cake:
Thinly ice the top of the bottom layer of the cake, then take the strawberries and place flat side down/pointy side up in concentric circles covering the bottom layer.

Pipe frosting between the strawberries (Ziploc bag with corner snipped off works fine as piping bag).

Place the other layer on top and ice top and sides. Garnish with fresh strawberries.

St. Louis Famous Gooey Butter Cake

Adapted from Molly Killeen and Melissa Clark

Take 3 tablespoons of milk at room temperature and 2 tablespoons of warm water and dissolve 2 teaspoons of yeast in it. Make sure it bubbles/foams.

Then cream 6 tablespoons of salted butter (room temp) with 2 tablespoons of granulated sugar. Scrape down the bowl and then beat in a large egg.

Now alternately beat in the yeast/milk mixture and 1¾ cups of all-purpose flour in 3 batches each. Scrape down the bowl after each addition. Beat this dough on medium until it is smooth and pulls away from the sides of the bowl.

Press the dough into an ungreased 9x13 baking dish and cover with plastic wrap and put in a warm spot. Allow it to rise until it has doubled...which should be between 2 and 3 hours.

After it has risen, heat the oven to 350 degrees.

Time to make the topping:
Use a small bowl and mix 3 heaping tablespoons of corn syrup (I prefer light) with 1 tablespoon warm water and 1 tablespoon of fresh-squeezed lemon juice.

Back to the mixer:
Cream together a stick and a half (12 tablespoons) of room-temperature salted butter and 1½ cups of granulated sugar until it is light and fluffy. Scrape down the bowl.

Now alternate the corn syrup mixture and a cup plus 3 tablespoons of all-purpose flour. Scrape down the sides of the bowl after each addition.

Spoon this topping over the risen mixture and use a spatula to spread it evenly over the top.

Bake. The cake will bake wavy on top. And it should be a golden brown when done. I bake mine for just under 40 minutes. Remember the gooey part. The center will still be "liquidy" when done, so no toothpick test.

Cool and then sprinkle lots of powdered sugar on top. Enjoy!

1234 Vanilla Cake

Adapted from the back of
the Swans Down cake flour box

Mix 12 ounces mascarpone with ½ cup fine sugar.

Then beat 3 cups of whipping cream with ½ cup fine sugar
and 1 teaspoon vanilla till stiff peaks.

Gradually fold that into the mascarpone. Ice first layer.

Put whole strawberries, points up, on the first layer.

Pipe the icing between the strawberries.

Then add the second layer. Ice all of the cake, leaving
the strawberries showing around the edges.
Pile strawberries on top!

Easy Hack for Bundt Cake

Preheat the oven to 325 degrees.

Mix together ¾ cup of vegetable oil, ½ cup of milk, and 1 cup of full-fat sour cream.

Next add 4 eggs.

Mix in 1 box cake mix and 1 box pudding mix.

Make sure to use plenty of baking spray in your Bundt cake pan or your Bundt mini-cake tins. Do not fill past two-thirds.

Start checking mini-cakes at 40 minutes. Full cakes tend to take closer to an hour.

Cake or mini-cakes should cool at least 15 minutes before turning out of the pan. When completely cool, add drizzle or glaze.

—Fmr. Sen. Claire McCaskill

BACKSPLASH

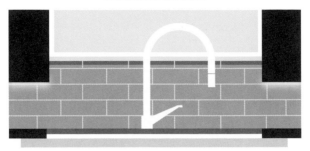

A backsplash is an area on a wall, usually in a bathroom or kitchen, that is covered in hard protective material. This is generally an upright, tiled surface behind a sink, countertop, or stove. Backsplashes are now used as much for decoration and contrast as they are for protecting walls, but the original ones were completely for function.

The first backsplashes came into use just after running water was invented in the 1930s and soon became common in kitchens and bathrooms everywhere. The early ones were small by today's standards, often only four inches high. By the 1950s, they became much more important as an item of décor instead of being merely functional. They started to be extended to cover the entire wall up to the cabinets. Over the next few decades, backsplashes started to be made from decorative tiles. Today, almost anything goes, and there are yearly trends as with all other types of home décor.

KNIFE BLOCK OR MAGNETIC STRIP?

People have strong feelings. Do you go with the knife block or mount a magnetic strip? Some feel the knife block is harder to keep clean. There is the fact that the knife block by necessity takes up valuable counter space. On the other hand, some people feel the magnetic strip may pose a possible safety hazard.

We are agnostic on the issue. Either is fine and better than keeping your knives in a drawer. Talk about a safety hazard!

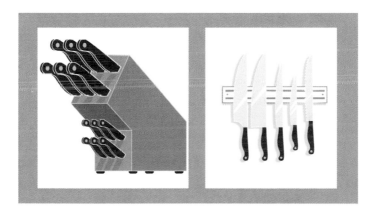

ROOM RATER TOP TIPS

ANA NAVARRO POLITICAL COMMENTATOR

Key components of a good room rating: lighting; décor, plant work, adorable pet. Lighting is crucial. Too much light, you look like Casper the Friendly Ghost. Too little light, you look like an unfriendly ghost. And too much backlighting, you look like you're sporting a halo. Décor requires a little punch of color, texture— and throw in a pillow or blanket or some sort of textile. Plants are your friends. They can hide all sorts of sins, a cord violation, a blank wall. I keep a lightweight planter of orchids that I can move around easily, depending on where I need it. When the real orchids die, I put in some silk ones. On TV, nobody can tell the difference. Put a note on your front door asking delivery folks not to knock. If the Amazon guy knocks on your door in the middle of a hit, all hell can break loose on live TV. My secret weapon is Chacha, my five-pound poodle. Having a live animal in frame is high-risk, high-reward. Be warned, once people see your pet, they're going to always want to see your pet. And next thing you know, she'll join the actors' union.

—Ana Navarro

The Classic Chair

We try to avoid making recommendations when doing so would involve your spending an inordinate amount of money. Unless you really want to. And can.

If you are able to make a single purchase, you might think of acquiring a classic chair to dramatically increase your video impact. No, not a chair to sit in—one to include behind you as part of your setup. The chairs on the list below are classic and in most cases have very distinctive profiles. They look good as furniture and for visual effect. We might even say chairs are art.

To be sure, in their original form these chairs tend to be pricey. The good news in almost every case is that a more reasonably priced reproduction is available and frankly recommended. As with art, we do not expect your Matisse to be original. Same with your classic chair.

Le Grand Confort/Corbusier

Leather Club Chair

Wingback Chair

Barcelona Chair

Windsor Chair

Rex Chair

Egg Chair

Swan Chair

Wassily Chair

Eames Lounge Chair

Therefore, here are the

ROOM RATER TOP TEN CLASSIC CHAIRS

10. Le Grand Confort/Corbusier

9. Leather club chair

8. Wingback chair

7. Barcelona chair

6. Windsor chair

5. Rex chair

4. Egg chair

3. Swan chair

2. Wassily chair

1. Eames lounge chair

Alternative Setup

STYLE #2

THE FIREPLACE

Tumultuous times have necessitated change in the way our society operates at the most basic level. We have adapted to the challenges of working from home and reshaped how we go about our daily lives. Home improvement projects now make more sense than ever before. Not only do we spend more time looking at our spaces, but so does everyone else, thanks to video calls.

The fireplace is a smart choice of background for those who have one. Fireplaces never go out of style and have become popular as the focal point of many rooms. There is something primal about the comfort and warmth a fireplace brings to a space. Even in the heat of summer, a fireplace can be a charming design element. Of course, a fireplace also tends to have the added benefit of a mantelpiece above it, providing a seamless display space for décor.

Early fireplaces were vital for heat and cooking. In the Stone Age, holes were dug in the ground and the day's hunt was grilled over an open flame. In medieval times, firepits were dug in the middle of the room, with a hole cut in the ceiling for the smoke. By the eleventh century, chimneys had been invented, so fireplaces moved from the middle of the room to an outside wall. This allowed for dwellings to be built on two or three levels. Eventually fireplaces became not just a practical means of obtaining heat, but the decorative centerpiece of the living room. In the Victorian era, upper-class households embellished their fireplaces with ornate engravings and decorated tiles.

In modern times, fireplaces have become more of an architectural feature than an essential item to heat your home. Whether gas or electric, brick and stone are still popular hearth-building materials; painting your fireplace a light color can also give it a modern and clean look. This can be tricky, because the shade you choose can make it stand out even more or blend into the rest of the room. Neutrals are a safe bet; they will work with any existing color scheme. A bright white can lighten the entire room, or a beige or off-white is a softer, warmer choice. We have also seen some great black fireplaces that make the room look sleek. If you are adventuresome, painting your fireplace a bright color will make it more of a standout.

Another trend in modern fireplaces is to go with new shapes as opposed to the traditional square model. Long, narrow fireplaces are rectangular, which creates a clean, minimalist look. Whether you choose to display art or a television above the mantel, a linear fireplace will complement this setup. On the other end of the scale, large square fireplaces are also popular if your space allows. Large hearths can make a room look elegant and become the centerpiece of any space. Some modern fireplaces also have convenient heat control options and even remote controls, so fireplaces can actually save you money as well as adding style to your home.

The Much-Discussed TV-Over-Fireplace Controversy

There are various concerns with having your television above a fireplace. In most cases, the television will be too high for comfortable viewing. Additionally, if you use your fireplace a lot, the heat that your television will be subject to could be damaging if not outright dangerous. Furthermore, this arrangement draws too much attention to the screen itself. We prefer a mirror, which will make the room look larger and reflect light or a large painting.

TOP TEN MANTEL DÉCOR ITEMS

1. Candles/candleholders
2. Vases
3. Souvenirs from your travels
4. Small artworks/sculptural pieces
5. Trophies/awards
6. Photos
7. Kids' art
8. Clocks
9. Plants
10. Flowers

ROOM RATER TOP NO-NOS

No-No #3: Taxidermy

Taxidermy. Don't go there. If it was alive and is now stuffed, it shouldn't be in public view. We don't care if that mounted buck was your grandpa's. In fact, that makes it worse.

Yes, that means no giant stuffed marlins. Fish art is great. But a mounted swordfish ain't it. No, not even at the cabin. No exceptions.

Musical Instruments

W e love all musical instruments and encourage you to incorporate them into your video backdrop. The best news of all: musicians are exempt from all cord violations. We enjoy music of all kinds and have had the pleasure of rating some great studios and talented musicians, both well known and new to us. Having your instrument on display humanizes you. As well as earning points with us, and taking the place of a plant, pet, or child, we have also found that a well-placed ukulele is a great conversation starter in the most serious of business meetings; who doesn't enjoy having a peek at what people do for fun?

We've seen exotic instruments from far-flung countries that are aesthetically beautiful objects of art in and of themselves. In many cases, these instruments tell a story as much as they function to create music. To be honest, even when they are displayed as decorations only, most viewers will assume someone in your house plays them and therefore has musical talent. We will always look favorably upon musical instruments in your Zoom room, so display them when you can, especially if you do not have access to a pet or child of your own or to borrow for the shot. And fear not if you do not have the space for a fancy baby grand piano in your living room; smaller instruments can score just as well. With any luck, no one will ask you for proof of any actual ability to play your displayed instruments.

ROOM RATER TOP TIPS

KATTY KAY BROADCAST JOURNALIST

Forget perfect. Matching pillows, lamps, and throws are fine in a hotel but look sterile in a home. Don't be afraid of a bit of humor or eccentricity—I'm fond of my childhood Tintin statue so he shows up in the shot. And—useful tip—for an easy punch of color try books with bright spines. Some people choose their TV books for the erudite content, I choose mine for their vivid blue, yellow, and red spines (useful hint to journalists hoping to get their books in shot?).

—Katty Kay

The Emergency Setup

I t happens. You're on the road, at a relative's home or at an undisclosed location. For whatever reason, the setup you normally use is unavailable. Children and pets are often the cause, but it can also be a spontaneous, last-minute emergency conference call or a breaking news story that allows little preparation time. Be ready. If you're on the road, have a backup plan. In your own home, it's a good idea to have a backup setup you can use if need be because you never know. Planes, trains, and automobiles will do in a pinch, but we suggest pulling over if you happen to be driving, because safety should always take precedence over having the perfect Zoom room.

Once you have your backup and temporary setup identified, make sure there are no red flags. Will there be enough light? Where is the best place for the camera? Are there any walls with large blank spaces? What about background noise? Try to correct the obvious flaws, but remember, most of us have been in this situation, so we suggest remembering the old adage: "Just do the best you can with what you have." Emergency sound blockers can include pillows and even towels if necessary. As well as pulling every lamp you own into your Zoom room, emergency light sources can include setting up near a window or skylight. We highly recommend tracking the direction of the sun so you can identify the best source of light. Do this a few times, and it will become second nature.

Top Ten Things to Check Before Your Appearance/Call

1. Check lighting: Do you have enough? Are there distracting reflections?
2. Is your camera/device at the right height?
3. Is your cell phone turned off or on silent mode?
4. Test all the technology that you will require for this call.
5. This might seem obvious, but looking directly into the camera equals making eye contact. The tendency on video calls is to look at yourself on the screen.
6. Turn off notifications.
7. Try to limit your body movements while you are speaking or looking into the camera. They can be distracting.
8. Feed your fluffy or feathered roommates if they tend to ask for their meal loudly.
9. Leave a note on your apartment/ house door asking folks to come back later.
10. Get out of your pajamas, at least from the waist up. And if there is a chance you will be standing at all, for the love of God, put on some pants.

ROOM RATER TOP TIPS

ERIN BROCKOVICH   AUTHOR, *SUPERMAN'S NOT COMING*

I like a little piece of Zen amid the chaos, which is why I light candles and bring in orchids (lots of them). Comfortable, inviting, and open, with a touch of something out of the ordinary. Old World meets New World kind of vibe. I bring home touches of other places I have been, but not too much, or it's overwhelming. And lots of natural light...After all, I am solar-powered!

—Erin Brockovich

The Great
HOLIDAY DECORATION DEBATE

DON CALLOWAY LAWYER

When does Christmas end? Let's be clear: we're talking about Christmas decorations and when they need to come down.

Not everyone is a Christian or celebrates Christmas. Not everyone who celebrates Christmas believes in decorating. But for those of us who do like to haul out the holly, we are obligated to engage with the all-important question: When do holiday decorations need to come down?

That is to say, how long after December 25 (or January 7 if you are of the Orthodox faith) should you pack all the garlands, icicles, bulbs, ornaments, and of course the tree itself for another year? Or another eleven months if you must.

While we understand that some people for a variety of practical reasons choose to go with an artificial tree, we feel this is a very personal decision often with religious undertones, so we are not necessarily advocating for live trees. However, that would be our choice.

Some people spend a great deal of time and effort—not to mention money—on their holiday setup. If you're going to have holiday décor in your background, you should at least be aware that after a certain point, people on your video call will begin to note that your Christmas tree is still up. You want to take it down before it seems out of place.

It would be unreasonable to expect a person, or a family, who spent so much time/effort decking the halls to undeck them immediately after Christmas, like the next day.

On the other hand, if you hardly do much decorating, aren't really into the holidays, and are just fine moving on, by all means feel free to pack it all in right away any day after the twenty-fifth.

We've seen extreme examples where decorations stay up

for months, and this is clearly unworkable. It's also a safety hazard, assuming you have a real Christmas tree. What's the right answer? We recommend any time up to about two weeks. Again, much sooner if that's your preference, but much longer than a couple of weeks and your remaining decorations will begin to seem out of place. Take a hint.

Let's also remember that the generally accepted start date to put up the decorations is the day after Thanksgiving—although many people will want to wait until well after December 1. Thus, if one decorates the last week of November and undecorates a full two weeks post-Christmas, that gives the festively inclined a full six weeks. That is more than enough.

Although rarer, the two-week takedown time frame can also apply to decorations relating to Chanukah, Kwanzaa, St. Patrick's Day, Valentine's Day, Arbor Day, and Independence Day.

Gnomes
Not Just Your Garden Variety

Gnomes have traditionally been garden décor, but they have been known to appear inside people's homes from time to time, and we embrace this migration. But they also have another role: In Scandinavia, gnomes represent Christmas, and the Scandinavian equivalent of Santa Claus is, in fact, a large gnome. During the holiday season, sightings of gnomes increase as they crawl out of storage and decorate homes across the land. We are solidly pro-gnome and believe that there should be both indoor and outdoor gnomery available, all year round.

Gnomes are mythological creatures, appearing first in oral traditions of European folklore, where they were depicted more as ugly goblins than the cherubic old codgers we see today. The gnomes of yore lived underground or deep in forests. Most European nations have a gnome story in their oral history and traditions. Over time and within different communities, gnomes have been given unique features, and examples of cultural variants remain to this day. However, one consistent trait pervades gnome lore: all gnomes have the ability to move swiftly underground.

The first garden gnomes appeared in Germany in the early 1800s. They were made of clay from molds and hardened in a kiln. The Germans believed that gnomes, along with trolls and fairies, lived in the forests. As opposed to the earlier depictions of them, these gnomes were happy little men with pointy hats and long beards, and often helped to guard property in their spare time.

When Sir Charles Isham traveled to Germany from England in 1847, he purchased twenty gnomes by the famous gnome sculptor Phillip Griebel (yes, that was a thing). He returned to England with these gnomes, and they quickly became a hot commodity all over Europe and eventually in North America. Anywhere where gardening was a hobby, they became common. They also became part of a subculture of collectors and have often been the object of pranks and kidnappings. In fact, Italy's MALAG (Garden Gnome Liberation Front) and France's Front de Libération des Nains de Jardins are groups that "liberate" garden gnomes.

Although some elite garden clubs have banned gnomes from their shows, gnomes have become popular in books, movies, video games, and even advertising.

The Nutcrackers: More Than a Ballet

One of the most popular traditional holiday decorations that has endured for centuries is the nutcracker. Those with strong nutcracker game score highly with us, and create a nostalgic, colorful background for their Zoom calls during the holidays.

The Nutcracker in History

Long before Tchaikovsky wrote the famous ballet that made nutcrackers synonymous with Christmas for so many, nutcrackers were a useful but uninteresting tool that looked like a pair of pliers. There are mentions of this tool being part of the table settings during family meals or while entertaining guests very early in European history.

The first wooden nutcrackers painted to resemble soldiers or knights date from the 1400s. In early German folklore, these nutcrackers were believed to protect your family against evil spirits and danger of all kinds. They were also believed to bring good luck and goodwill to the household.

When the ballet *The Nutcracker* became a hit in North America in the 1950s, nutcrackers became a popular holiday accessory and a prized collectible item (the ballet is set during Christmas and stars—you guessed it—a nutcracker, so the two remain entwined to this day).

Some say the staying power of nutcrackers is due to the overall trend in decorating with vintage pieces. They remain easily identifiable in homes and can add a touch of festivity to any setting.

The Pineapple
A FRUIT STORY

The pineapple may mean different things to different people, but it has long been a part of the history of home décor. When Columbus landed in the Caribbean, his crew saw that pineapples were hung outside the homes of the islands' Indigenous people to indicate that they welcomed strangers. Once the pineapples made their way back to Europe with the ship crews, they became popular with the upper classes. They also became a decorating design for colonial houses and plantations in the southern United States. To this day, the pineapple symbol is used in the hospitality industry worldwide.

For centuries, the pineapple was also considered exotic by everyone who was unfamiliar with the fruit. And because pineapples were so difficult to grow in much of the world, they became so valued that the well-off did not eat them—they just displayed them for guests as a sign of their prosperity. People who could not grow them could rent them, and theft of pineapples became common. Artists were commissioned to paint the fruit. Eventually, increased importation brought pineapples to the mainstream, and their association with the rich members of society began to lessen. But pineapples have retained their reputation as a symbol of hospitality all over the world. It is now commonplace to see pineapple motifs on pillows, fabrics, ceramics, and glass, and to see the fruit hanging on walls in still lifes.

An extravagant example of the pineapple used in art and architecture is the Dunmore Park house in Scotland.

This huge stone pineapple is the best-known building on the estate of the earls of Dunmore. It was built in 1761 by the fourth earl as a present for his wife. After the family moved out in 1911, it eventually became part of the National Trust for Scotland. Today, it can be rented out for accommodation or events.

Kids and Photobombs

IRWIN REDLENER, MD MSNBC ANALYST, CHILD ADVOCATE AND AUTHOR

Children's photobombs are easily our most requested and liked Zoom room enhancers. We have seen dozens of video clips and shots of babies, toddlers, youngsters, and even a few teenagers bursting into rooms during live meetings.

We all love to see them now, but it should be noted that this wasn't always the case: here's one example of how our opinions as viewers have evolved over time.

Flash back to April 2020. The pandemic was gaining momentum all across the world. Getting people set up from home became the norm for office workers everywhere, and even broadcasters began setting up home offices. As we began to see glimpses of how "those people on TV" lived, it was fun and it gave us a sense of well-being and camaraderie; we were all in this together, including laundry, messy spaces, and, of course, children and pets. We all could relate, and as we saw more of this on our screens, it became our new normal.

The early kids' photobombs were met with mixed reactions; not everyone liked them. Some said it was distracting and "unprofessional" to have one's children bursting into the room or deal with a cranky toddler on-screen. But as time went on and people began to realize that many of us would be home for some time to come, attitudes shifted. By the summer, our kid and pet interruptions became some of our more popular tweets.

With many countries adopting a hybrid of office/home work, the inevitability of household members dropping in unannounced isn't going to stop anytime soon. Our suggestion is simple when it comes to children: bring them on! We all have our moments where our work is rudely interrupted by the outside world, where our carefully curated professional versions of ourselves are upended by forces beyond our control. There is no use pretending to be immune to the distractions of home, so best embrace it. Seeing our coworkers' children can bring some much-needed levity to otherwise monotonous meetings. Our best advice: Let the children play. And relax. We are all in this together.

Alternative Setup
STYLE #3

THE ATTIC

The finished attic setup is a good option for those with larger households where a degree of privacy is desired. If you share a household with noisy occupants, as many of us with offspring do, the attic may be your best bet to insulate you from any potentially embarrassing or distracting commotion.

These spaces tend to be smaller and are usually marked by the presence of slanted walls. The walls can prove challenging, as it's hard to mount normal wall art at an angle. Lighting is key. You'll want to make sure there's plenty, as it will help open up the space.

A slanted wall can often accommodate a three- or four-foot bookcase, while the interior wall may be a good spot for a full-height bookcase.

DORMER WINDOWS

Dormer windows are windows that both have their own roofs and are located on the slope of a roof or a wall. The roof of the dormer window can come in many shapes and styles, such as arched, "eyebrow," gabled, or polygonal. Dormers can let in extra light and warmth, and make an excellent architectural feature. We most often see these in the attic setup.

Violation #2

THE LAMP SEAM VIOLATION

L et's start with the basics. What is a lamp seam violation? Technically, it's short for lampshade seam violation. Lamp seam violation, or LSV, for brevity's sake.

An LSV occurs when any seam on a lampshade can be seen. Having a visible lamp seam is distracting but easily remedied.

To be clear, LSV applies to your normal round or oval shade. Before your Zoom, double-check. Is the lamp on? Usually the answer should be yes. Good, but you're not done yet. It's so easy, it will become second nature to check. Where's the lampshade seam? Make sure it faces away from the camera and you're done. Just get used to making this quick but vital check and the lamp seam violation need never be an issue at all. And that is how it should be.

We tend to be absolutists on LSVs, unlike with the broader and more common cord violations, which can at times be waived or so minor that they can be overlooked. (See "Violation #1: The Cord Violation" for specific instances.)

It is important to note that certain lampshades—often square or rectangular shades—have four seams; in such cases, it is normal—and indeed impossible to avoid—to have at least one seam showing. Occasionally, we will see a round or oval lampshade with three seams. As with four-seamed shades, these are exempt from the LSV.

Globes

RICHARD HAASS   COUNCIL ON FOREIGN RELATIONS PRESIDENT

W hy globes? Here are ten reasons, in addition to the fact that my wife, Susan, likes shopping for them, in part because they solve the problem of what to get me when a present seems in order. What's more, as a former television producer, she is particularly well suited to arranging them, which in no small part explains why Room Rater noticed and thought well of what I was up to:

1. It's important to stay on brand, and my day job is to analyze what is happening around the globe and explain what it means for the United States.

2. Globes are a useful reference, as they are more accurate than maps, which distort distances and arbitrarily place some regions at the center and others at the periphery.

3. With all due respect to whoever coined the phrase "History is about chaps and geography maps," you cannot understand history without appreciating geography.

4. Globes of the world are a late-fifteenth-century invention, coming only after the ideas that the earth was flat and the sun revolved around it were proven to be false. I am reminded of such debates when I hear climate change deniers and vaccine skeptics.

5. I loved going to the 1964 New York World's Fair when I was barely a teenager and seeing the Unisphere, a giant metallic globe exhibition.

6. I still love seeing the Unisphere except when I am stuck in traffic (usually trying to catch a flight) looking at it.

7. There are days when I feel a bond with Atlas (condemned to hold up the world), when I do battle with isolationists and others who refuse to accept how what goes on elsewhere in the world matters to the United States.

8. Globes are what the earth looks like from space, or so I'm told. For all sorts of reasons, I do not expect to be channeling what little inner Jeff Bezos or Elon Musk I may possess, so staring at these globes is as close as I'll get to looking down from the outside.

9. It is fun to try to date old globes by looking at what countries existed when they were made.

10. Globes are art.

Room Rater

PICK-A-STYLE

Picking a new place, are you lucky enough to be able to pick a style? If you are, here's a brief overview of a few of our favorites.

MIDCENTURY MODERN   A great option if you inherited some items from your parents or grandparents that date back to the fifties and sixties—you're already halfway there! This style is described as functional and understated, and is characterized by clean lines and streamlined forms. Instantly recognizable examples include the Herman Miller chair and the Eames lounge chair.

COUNTRY CHIC This look combines rustic, weathered, and distressed pieces, pastel colors, and vintage furniture. If you enjoy garage and yard sales, this could be a great way to incorporate this style inexpensively.

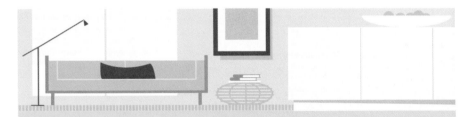

SCANDINAVIAN Sleek. Cool. If you enjoy hours of trying to put together furniture from a box, this approach is perfect for you. Characteristics include minimalist, neutral color palette, clean lines, modern, and blends of textures.

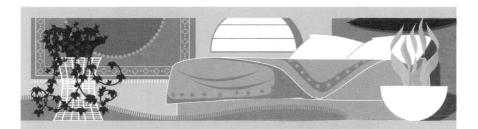

BOHEMIAN   You don't need to find some tie-dye and Birken-stocks for this one, although we certainly won't discourage you. Think bright colors, pieces from faraway countries, and eclectic décor with lots of patterns and rich, saturated colors.

INDUSTRIAL   Everyone wants to live in a converted warehouse or a loft with exposed brick or original beams, but there are ways to get the industrial feel in a small place. Select décor made of materials like wood, steel, and stone, neutral tones, and straight lines.

LIZA YUZDA LEGISLATIVE REPORTER

Creativity is key to keeping it fresh—and to pandering to your audience. With humor. My "piece of art" wall has been a great space to rotate canvases with different messages each week. Hiding any mess in a room might also hold the key. So, find a corridor of your room that has some interesting elements—lamps, plants, objets d'art—and make sure any clutter is on the other side of the camera.

—Liza Yuzda

More on Lamps

B y now, we have established that if there is a lamp in your shot, in nearly all cases it should be switched on. Depending on the time of day, this may have little to no impact on your actual lighting—but it will keep you from looking like you're in a depressed, cryptlike environment. Often, you just need enough light to light up the shade if there is one. In other cases, you will want as much light as any bulb can manage.

In most cases you have the lamp or lamps you need, and you just need to turn them on. If you determine that you need more pieces for your setup, there are lots of affordable choices. There are also lots of very pricey ones. Find a basic floor lamp for the living room setup. There are any number of table lamps that will add to desk setups. One of our favorite lamp styles is the classic leg lamp, but we recommend picking one that says something about your own personal style.

ROOM RATER TOP NO-NOs

No-No #4: Digital Backgrounds

We don't do digital backgrounds and neither should you. If you picked up this book in a bookstore and are committed to using green screen/digital backgrounds, put the book down and walk away. It's not for you. We are about making your real-life environment look as good as possible. No. There is no compromise. What you are doing is wrong and makes you look funny. Digital backgrounds look artificial and feel like you are trying to put one over on your audience. You should stop and rethink your life.

O Canada, Eh?

STEWART REYNOLDS   @BRITTLESTAR

R oom Rater is half Canadian, and Canadian content plays a large role on our account. We met Brittlestar, or as he is known to family and close personal friends, Stewart Reynolds. His political and pandemic-related PSAs made us laugh, and sometimes cry, but always think. And speaking of Canada and Reynolds, the other one, Ryan, also did very well in our ratings. We rated the rooms of actors, politicians, musicians, and journalists.

We saw uniquely Canadian items displayed, like Hudson's Bay items, Tim Hortons coffee, hockey memorabilia, and the Tragically Hip music. We rated the prime minister's room often, and although he has yet to formally thank us, we appreciate how he took some of our advice to heart. Followers from around the world have likely learned that Canadians are super nice, and say "eh" and "sorry" too much, but our passive-aggressiveness is strong. And for that, we Canadians are very sorry.

Aside from the fun, there was also a feeling that we were all in this pandemic together. As most of the world went into some sort of lockdown, it comforted us to see ourselves as part of a global community. Even though our worlds became smaller as we moved inside, we could still use the internet to connect to people far away.

TOP TIPS

The Quintessential Canadian room requires no specific decoration or objet d'art.

Nor does it require literal demonstration of the cultural mosaic that is Canada.

No, the key to the perfect Canadian room background is what's not in the frame.

A gun, for example. Yeah, if you want your room to look Canadian, don't put a gun in the frame.

Alternative Setup

STYLE #4

THE BEDROOM

The bedroom setup is a viable option for many. There are some who feel strongly that bedrooms are private, or they should be, and don't want to see yours and will not show you theirs. That's fine. We take no position other than to say that if you want to shoot in your bedroom, you are free to do so. If you'd rather not, then don't. Most people will have other options, like a kitchen setup, for example, or a basic bookcase setup.

Clearly, hotel room setups are permissible and necessary, because that's reality for most people some of the time, and hotel rooms are, by definition, bedrooms.

Leaving the controversy over the bedroom setup aside, let's deal with facts. It's a room and there's a bed. That bed must be neatly made. You'd think that would go without saying, but...we'll just say it again. One must present a reasonably well-made bed. One doesn't need to obsess over hospital corners, just make the bed as if a great many will see it, because perhaps they will. Related is to not have any piles of laundry on the neatly made bed.

Pillows should be in their normal flat position. This goes for typical bedroom pillows used for sleeping, not decorative pillows, which should be upright. How many decorative pillows to use is a question of personal taste and style; in most cases, three or four may be considered overkill. On the other hand, if you have a nice comforter or a sharp bedspread in the closet, this is a good time to make use of it.

Violation #3
THE RING LIGHT VIOLATION

This is perhaps the least significant of the Room Rater violations. It is also easily avoidable, and usually a slight repositioning of your ring light is all it takes.

Let's start with some definitions. There are two general types of ring light violations (RLVs). The first type is when part or the whole of your circular ring light can be seen reflected by a surface behind you. Most commonly the ring light reflection (full circle or crescent) can be seen mirrored on a framed piece of artwork, diploma, or something similar. This can be managed in most cases by a slight adjustment in the ring light's positioning. In some cases, the offending RLV is more subtle, with the ring light reflection visible on a shiny kitchen cabinet, another surface, or even the wall itself. Again, a slight adjustment will take care of the problem.

The more troublesome RLVs are of course when the ring light is seen reflected in the subject's glasses. It may seem unfair to single out those of us who wear glasses, and perhaps it is. But if you choose to wear glasses, certain realities go with the territory. For example, there are times when your eyeglasses will fog up. It happens. You deal with it. Same is true with Zoomers who have added a ring light to improve their lighting but wear glasses. If this applies to you, you must simply check before your meeting, YouTube, or TV hit: can we see your ring lights in your spectacles? As with RLV reflected on surfaces behind you, you simply need to check. As a general rule for eyeglass wearers, we recommend using the ring light at a slight angle—not directly in front of you.

DR. NAHID BHADELIA — FOUNDING DIRECTOR, BOSTON UNIVERSITY CENTER FOR EMERGING INFECTIOUS DISEASES

It's all about light and dimension. When you have an open space behind you, you have more room to personalize and create depth. Having a natural source of light in the room gives the frame variety over the course of the day. Also, always keep cat treats close at hand in case your media-seeking feline finds her way out of a closed door ready to bounce into the frame.

—Dr. Nahid Bhadelia

Setup Style #4

THE TWO-ROOM SETUP

The two-room setup is a good option if you're fortunate enough to have a larger house or apartment and want to maximize the depth of your background. You will still be positioned near the camera, but viewers will be able to see farther into your house.

Many different two-room combinations are possible, depending on the size of your home, but we will deal with just a few.

One of the best options if you have both a living room and a separate dining room is to shoot from one into the other.

In general, we've found that sitting in a dining room chair in the dining room with one wall or art behind you and with a view into the living room is classic and inviting. Conversely, you can sit in the living room in a chair positioned so that we see across the room into the dining room. This is often both a good way to showcase your interesting furniture and a chance to show more art, as it gives you more wall to work with.

As always, lighting is key, and each space must have its own. Never shoot from a lit room into a darkened next room, as the second room will be an unappealing void. On the other hand, if you light the second room, it can become an overall positive and make the entire setup look deeper and more interesting. If you don't want to show the living room beyond the dining room, use another composition. If you do show an additional room, you must light it. It must have its own combination of lighting—lamps, and in some cases overhead lighting.

The kitchen-into-the-dining-room view or vice versa is as American as Mom's apple pie. Which you can place in the dining room or on the kitchen island. The dining room offers a good place to show off your table centerpiece, if you have one. Don't have one? Put a $20 bouquet of flowers from Safeway in a decent-looking vase, and you'll achieve the same or better results. Put some fruit in a bowl on the kitchen counter and give it a whirl. Yes. Leave the blender.

WE LOVE FRENCH DOORS

A French door can be described as any hinged or swinging door made mainly of glass. French doors look and function as half window, half door by letting light in while providing privacy. For small spaces, sliding French doors are an option. They also connect rooms and create depth.

The origin of French doors really is in France, during the French Renaissance in the seventeenth century. This was before electricity, so the glass let in much-needed light. French doors were commonly used as tall windows leading onto small patios. And since glass was very expensive, they became a symbol of affluence and prestige.

Eventually, French doors came to England and then North America, where they remain popular indoors and out. Aside from aesthetics and the light they provide, they are also an excellent ventilation source because they swing open and can catch breezes. Consider them a sound investment.

TOP 25 DÉCOR ITEMS

1. Pineapples

2. Plants

3. Flowers

4. Globes

5. Sports memorabilia

6. Fruit bowls

7. Lego models

8. Old cameras

9. Vases

10. Clocks

11. Telescopes

12. Candles

13. Bar carts/bars

14. Model ships

15. Model rockets, especially the *Saturn 5*

16. Toy tractors

17. Action figures/bobbleheads

18. Old bottles/colored glass

19. Old radios

20. Old mics

21. Lava Lamps

22. Saddles

23. Classic toys

24. Classic lunch boxes

25. Fish art

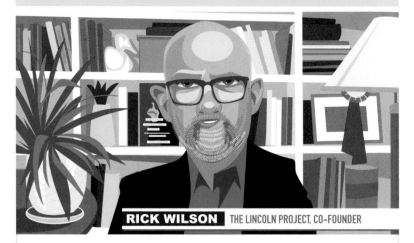

RICK WILSON THE LINCOLN PROJECT, CO-FOUNDER

It has been strange to peek into the lives of the chattering class, in which I somehow find myself from time to time.

In my case, you can see we're dog people, horse people, and book people. I've had a few viewers try to analyze the books behind me. Those sections are mostly folklore and philosophy, not politics, so maybe a little strategic reorganization is due.

And yes, the pineapples were hella deliberate!

—Rick Wilson

Window Treatments

Drapes   Curtains   Roman

Mini blinds   Vertical blinds   Sheers

How we dress our windows is so much more than our personal taste, aesthetically. Window treatments can make a big difference to a room's light, temperature, privacy, and security as well. The choices can be confusing, but here are some basics to consider. There are three types of window coverings: soft, hard, and a hybrid of the two.

SOFT WINDOW TREATMENTS   As the name suggests, these are made with soft materials/fabrics. Some examples are curtains, drapes, sheers, Roman shades, and valances.

HARD WINDOW TREATMENTS   These are made of hard materials. Some examples are shutters, blinds, and shades.

A SOFT/HARD COMBINATION   Think of Roman blinds made with wood.

The right fit is a matter of personal priorities. Most people care a great deal about how light their rooms/homes are. Work back from whatever you need or want; hard treatments and dark, thick fabrics will block the sun and reduce heat, while the soft, light-colored ones will let more light in.

A couple of obvious points: darker and heavier window treatments in the bedroom can help you sleep. In other rooms, maximizing natural light is always a winning approach. We saw curtains, drapes, and the other soft styles become increasingly popular during the pandemic for this exact reason. Controlling the heat can also play a role in your decision on window treatment. Whatever function you want your window coverings to perform, you will have a multitude of options in terms of styles and materials.

ROMAN SHADES/BLINDS These are horizontal shades that when opened (with a drawstring) compress in an even stack, and when closed have a smooth surface. They are classic and never go out of style. They can be made of many materials, even wood. They are great at keeping heat out or in, can filter or block light, and offer privacy because of their large single sheets. Many modern models are motorized, so they are safe for pets and small tots because they pose no safety hazard.

WOODEN SHUTTERS With rustic chic being popular and a back-to-nature trend in home décor, wooden shutters are a great choice. Among the biggest advantages is the sound insulation, so shutters are ideal for homes in noisy cities. They are cost-efficient as well, and will save you money for heating your room in winter. They also shield from sunlight when needed, are easy to clean and care for, and add privacy. An investment in shutters will add value to your home.

Many people do not have the luxury of floor-to-ceiling windows. While keeping in mind the importance of maximizing the light from any source, use sheer curtains or drapes on your windows. You can fake having taller and larger windows by hanging the sheers from the ceiling and letting them hang all the way to the floor instead of just covering the actual windows. This trick can work wonders for small spaces.

TRANSOM

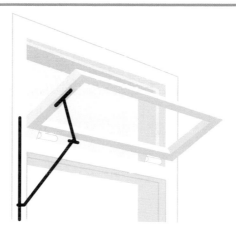

Transoms are an attractive architectural feature seen in some older homes and even some classic city apartments. The name refers to a kind of window located over the crosspiece above the door. Technically, this crosspiece is called a transom, but in architectural terms, the transom often refers to the window above it. The window is usually rectangular, but in some instances can be fan shaped.

A transom or transom window is not to be confused with the vertical reinforcement that strengthens the stern of a boat.

Many people have heard the term in publishing. The expression is slang for an unsolicited manuscript, one tossed 'over the transom,' as it were. Additionally, in journalism, this term can refer to information received from anonymous sources.

Add a Classic Touch

Classic typewriters send a message. You're bookish. You read a lot of Hemingway. You know who Edward R. Murrow was. You're a journalist, a reporter, or perhaps a novelist. No one expects the typewriter to work—that's not the point. If this were seventy years ago, you'd be heading to a war zone with your portable Smith-Corona tucked under your arm. Ask not for whom the bell tolls.

In the meantime, the old manual typewriter looks good when placed strategically on a mid-low shelf. Perhaps on a corner of the desk. We can work with exact placement but not front and center. It's a set piece but a good one. Never mind that you're more comfortable in Google Docs and couldn't change a ribbon if your life depended upon it even if they were still being made.

If typewriters aren't your thing, maybe you have your grandparents' Brownie or your dad's 35mm camera. Folks see you're out there in the world capturing it all. This is the camera that captured your sixth birthday party. Okay. Or your mom's. Or it's a camera just like it. The distinction is that the old/vintage or antique camera was a film camera. Analog. Retro. Pre-digital. And that's what makes it cool.

Unlike manual typewriters, we often find older cameras displayed in twos and threes. Sometimes grouped together, but more often distributed throughout a multishelf book setup. This can be a most pleasing effect. Tom Hanks is a notable exception—he often appears in interviews with his typewriter collection.

Album covers make for great displays. The standard LP jacket measures fifteen by fifteen inches, and for some decades in the mid-to-late twentieth century, some of the best popular art and photography could be found on albums. Sometimes heavy metal. Classic rock is more likely. Jazz and blues in a lot of rooms, too. A record collection is instantly recognizable by its size, if not by its artwork. Can you have a respectable collection of albums without a turntable? Yes, but you may open yourself up to being seen as a bit of a poser.

Some will want to think about adding a classic piece of sports memorabilia. Baseball cards are nice but don't have

much visual impact due to their small size. Baseballs are just large enough to be displayed in specially made cases or just as they are.

If you want to go all out, think jerseys. Old, famous teamwear can add a classic feel to a room. Have them professionally box framed for proper presentation. Footballs and basketballs have their appeal. A Louisville Slugger will not go amiss.

There are many classic toys that can be positioned for décor points. Some of the most popular are Rubik's Cubes, Buzz Lightyear, and any number of *Sesame Street* characters.

By contrast, for sheer visual impact it's hard to beat some of the larger modern Lego sets. Among these, the most popular are the *Star Wars* series. Canadian prime minister Justin Trudeau has a battle cruiser prominently displayed in his most often seen room.

JEMELE HILL STAFF WRITER, *THE ATLANTIC*

Never in a million years would I have ever imagined myself as someone who cared one iota about the décor in my home office, but these challenging times have brought out my inner Martha Stewart. I became obsessed specifically with bookshelves because that's ultimately what makes an office sing. So in order to have a bookshelf that sings, I suggest building a bookshelf display around items that show your personality and give people a window into who you are. The one item on my bookshelf that always sparks a conversation is my beloved San Francisco 49ers helmet. Now, this isn't just any old helmet. The helmet was not only autographed by both Dwight Clark and Joe Montana, but even better, the famous play "The Catch"—which is the game-winning touchdown play they made in 1981's NFC Championship Game— is diagrammed on the top of the helmet. I have a ton of books, but the ones I display so they can be prominently seen are written by dear friends of mine. It's my way not only of showcasing their work, but also of telling them how proud I am of them for such a monstrous achievement. So, when it comes to designing a great bookshelf, think personality and authenticity first.

—Jemele Hill

MICHAEL SCHMIDT REPORTER,
THE NEW YORK TIMES

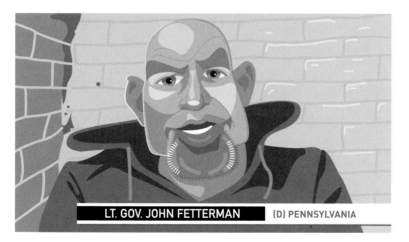

LT. GOV. JOHN FETTERMAN (D) PENNSYLVANIA

The Hostage Video

I t's the end of March 2020. Everyone has gone into lock-down and people are worried about where their next roll of toilet paper is coming from. Suddenly, everyone is on cable doing TV hits from home. Your boss is texting "Can you join us at 3:30?" You say yes. How hard can it be? You have Zoom. You got this. You set up the laptop and aim up at the blank wall behind you. You may not know it, but you just fell victim to the hostage video setup. Typically, these are shot far too low, granting us the "full nostril view" as a bonus. Early on, many people took this route. But what you put behind you is as important as and will be remembered longer than what you put forward. We still see this setup, but most people have long since realized that plants, books, print, pooch, or pine-apple—it's easy to organize your own rescue mission.

ROOM RATER TOP TIPS

DR. VIN GUPTA   NBC NEWS MEDICAL CONTRIBUTOR

I never used to think about the space behind me, mainly just about lighting when I could control it. Which can be hard when you take a TV segment hit from inside a hospital ward or intensive care unit, as I often do. Those settings are bleak, often with white backgrounds and no decorations. It wasn't until my first 4/10 "hostage room" rating from Room Rater that I realized background matters; it can be distracting for viewers if it's terrible, and can dilute or completely overshadow the message you're trying to deliver. So I iterated; I sought expert counsel from my wife—who should be an interior decorator—and actually put some effort into making the wall behind me somewhat pleasant to look at. After a Lowe's trip to get my favorite-hue-of-blue bucket of paint, a required West Elm trip to get some fancy framing, and a Barnes & Noble trip to get the required book, *The Great Influenza*, by John M. Barry, to place behind me as a COVID communicator, I knew I was well on my way to a 10/10.

—Dr. Vin Gupta

Alternative Setup

STYLE #5

THE FINISHED BASEMENT

In many homes, the finished basement is a great place to teleconference. The finished basement is typically set up as a home office, den, or family room. As with the attic setup, one principal advantage of the finished basement is privacy. Typically, it's fairly easy to ensure that the kids and pets don't interrupt your video call—although it's just peachy if they do.

One sometimes unavoidable issue with finished basements is that they tend to be fairly low-ceilinged. You'll want to take this into account, as in general we don't really want to see much of your ceiling unless it's exceptional. If you do have a drop ceiling, as many finished basements do, you'll want to ensure that it is not visible in the frame.

DROP CEILING

Sometimes called a dropped ceiling, a drop ceiling is a secondary ceiling built below the main one. It can also be referred to as a suspended ceiling, false ceiling, or T-bar ceiling. These features seem to be either loved or hated, but rarely anything in between.

Drop ceilings date back to the 1300s in Japan. They also were popular in England from the 1500s as a feature to improve acoustics in theaters. The first drop ceilings were seen in the US beginning in 1919. They provided a way to hide the inner workings of a building and to allow easy access to make repairs to pipes and wiring. Larger multiunit dwellings often used them to conceal sprinkler systems. However, drop ceilings do make the ceiling lower, so if you are tall, this might not be a good option for you.

Camera Height

Whether you are using an outdated smartphone, a fancy tablet, an intricate laptop, or a traditional camera, the importance of camera height cannot be overstated. This is an error we see all the time, and it can be the difference between a 2/10 and a 10/10. The good news? It is one of the easiest fixes to make, and we will show you how.

The easiest way to discern whether your camera is positioned too low is to determine if the viewer can see your nostrils. No one needs to see those. Another indication is if we the viewers can see your ceiling; unless that ceiling is spectacular, like James Carville's, we do not need to see that either. (Please note, if given the choice, we'd rather see the ceiling than the nostrils.)

Basically, you must use the "whatever it takes" approach to finding the optimum camera height. An easy and common fix is books. We don't just love books for reading, and many people overlook their utilitarian aspect. Stack them up—hardcovers, softcovers, textbooks, magazines, or a mix. Usually, it takes a variety of book styles to achieve optimal camera position height. What you stack the books on will vary greatly as well. We have seen cat perches (we admit to using this ourselves), small appliances, boxes, and all types of furniture become makeshift tripods. Remember, much as with what you are or are not wearing from the waist down, we cannot see what you decide to use for the camera stand, so the possibilities are endless. Just make sure the surface is stable.

If you are using an object belonging to a pet or a child (or spouse) as part of your jerry-rig, try to let them know so there won't be any surprises during the call.

However it is that you've chosen to create your shot, the goal should always be to have the camera squared at your eye level. Practice makes perfect, and it helps to have someone take a few shots of you first. And whatever you do, make sure you remember exactly how you achieved the perfect height, so you will be ready for the next video call. We suggest taking a picture of the setup when you get it right.

FRESH & TASTY PIZZA

Alternative Setup

STYLE #6

THE HOTEL

We rate rooms. Your room. The room you're in. It matters not if it's your folks' place, your sister's place, or, yes...a hotel room. All are fair game. In some cases, a borrowed room may be an improvement. In any case, Room Rater doesn't concern itself with who owns the room. New or used. Bought or borrowed. We judge you where you are.

Hotels happen. We all need them. It follows, therefore, that some Zooming is going to happen from hotels...so remember the basics and it can turn out well. First off—just because your location is a temporary one, there is no reason to subject your friends, family, associates, or audience to a view up your nostrils. As in your home setup, it's important to get the camera height to the correct level in a hotel room.

A couple of suggestions. You probably don't have a stack of books handy on the road, so depending on height needed, a hotel trash bin or ice bucket can work wonders. Be creative. Work the problem. It's worth it. We often rate the rooms of people who get camera height right at home but who tend to slip with temporary setups. That's unfortunate and unnecessary.

Once you get the height you need, you next need to consider the background itself.

It's a hotel. How bad is the art? What's the lamp situation?

The key question is: Are you going to go with a lamp/couch shot (if there's a couch), or will the bed be in the background? If you're going with a shot that includes the bed, you must 100 percent make sure the bed is neatly made. We cannot stress this enough. We are not opposed, as some are, to having a bed in your shot; just please do not ever let us see an unmade bed, whether at home or on the road.

Two of the most important elements in a hotel setup are the lamp and the curtains. Both can be used to your advantage. Remember: in nearly every case, you'll want the lamp on. If your hotel has a longish wall with art/lamp/chair or couch, perhaps try a setup that shoots down the wall at an angle. We recommend sitting in the desk chair rather than going for the couch view. (See "The Couch View.")

To pull off a decent hotel setup, try to re-create the shot you'd set up if you were home. Decide on your angle. Try to incorporate some curtains in your shot (if they aren't dreadful). Remember to turn the lamp on. Try not to include a distinctly hotel air conditioning system. We know you're in a hotel. The important thing is to make it look natural, comfortable, and as aesthetically pleasing as possible.

Lighting

Reflected · Natural · Under cabinet · Natural · Accent · Ring · Background

O ne would think that lighting would be straightforward when it comes to setting up a Zoom room background. Just add light, right? That seems like the most logical and obvious rule of thumb. And sometimes it is. However, the type of light, the time of day, the angle of the light, and the positioning of the lighting you choose are all important factors to consider. Your lighting choices will also affect other elements in the room, so (no pressure!) in a way your lighting is the very foundation of a well-curated room. The good news is that you do not need to spend a lot of money on items like ring lights and studio lighting, although we will speak about this a bit. Items you already have in your home can be used to create a well-lit space; you may need to move lamps from other rooms into your Zoom room, but it is well worth it.

Natural Light

Natural light is the preferred light source, one might think. And yes, at certain times of day, at certain angles, this is absolutely correct. A room awash with morning light from a window sounds lovely. The problem is, it can also lead to back-lighting issues, in which too much light from behind results in a washed-out visual effect. But yes, by all means, seek out a natural light source when possible. Here are some tips on making the most of this enviable asset:

Remember that the goal is to have a soft light framing your face—that will be the most important aspect to nail. Facing a window is always best, because sitting directly in front of one may cause you to become backlit. Too much backlight results in you and the rest of the room appearing to be washed out in a strange otherworldly halolike effect. A quick note on this: we have seen this work under some conditions, but it is dependent on time of day and angle of sun, so it can be tricky and generally should be avoided.

Use What You've Got

Even among those of us who have access to a natural light source in our Zoom room, not all have control over the time of day our call or interview is. Four a.m. on the West Coast is still pitch-dark, no matter how much natural light your room has. So what can you do when your office or video room has no source of natural light? You create your own light—and lots of it! Whatever it takes, and sometimes it takes bringing in every table and floor lamp in your house. (Just be careful to avoid the dreaded lamp seam violation!) Here are some tips from what we have seen and even what we have done for our own interviews and Zoom calls:

The biggest tip for nonnatural light is to keep it gentle. Harsh, bright lights are not flattering to you or your room. Start with a lamp or light fixture, preferably with LED lighting, that you can place behind your camera and aim at a spot behind where you sit, making sure it lights up your entire face; uneven lighting can be distracting. Next, if needed, add side light, again keeping it gentle. Moving the light sources farther back can help keep the brightness to a minimum. Overhead lighting and backlighting can be tricky, so if you can get away with side and front lighting, so much the better. This could be either on-camera in the form of a lamp or from a light source off-camera.

Remember, as with many aspects of Zoom room setups, balance is essential. As far as lighting goes, multiple sources of light are always better than one. Ideally, one source will illuminate the subject (you), and this needs to be balanced with equal light on either side of your frame.

A word about lightbulbs: First, always and forever avoid yellow and bright when choosing bulbs. Whether you choose LED or any other type of bulb, a good rule of thumb for the most flattering videos is to keep them as close to natural light as possible. One way to soften and diffuse light is to place a paper lantern around overhead lighting. In a pinch, wax or tissue paper can act as a DIY diffuser. These are very inexpensive hacks that can be very effective.

Desk lamps are another relatively inexpensive tip. For more professional lighting items, ring lights do not have to run you hundreds of dollars; there are many affordable models on the market. Just be careful with reflections! (See Violation #3: The Ring Light Violation.) We have seen some very distracting do-nut shapes on walls and foreheads. LED panel lighting is also an option, and this can range in price. Inexpensive lighting kits are available online.

The bottom line: Re-create natural light when you do not have it. Research lighting products that illuminate you and your space and put you in the very best possible light.

Table Lamp   Floor Lamp   Desk Lamp   Ring Light

What to Wear

Room Rater has always had a policy that we do not rate attire. And we will continue to uphold that guiding principle, but we can talk about the colors of that apparel. From a Zoom call point of view, a general rule is that solid, deeper, richer tones will show up better on a small screen. Avoid white, except as an accent. White and other lighter colors like pastels, and especially small prints against a light background, will tend to get lost. Basic shades like black, browns, grays, and darker blues are easy choices, but deep reds and bright yellows also work well. Also note, if you are using a green screen, avoid wearing any shade of green lest your torso disappear!

Patterns can be problematic. Repeating patterns such as chevrons, houndstooth, stripes, and plaid can be distracting and create tricks of the eye that will make you look like you are moving. The last thing you need is your boss feeling nauseated when you are speaking.

Another tip is to avoid wearing any color that is too similar to or that clashes with your background; if you have mostly neutrals in your Zoom room, wearing neutrals will mean you get lost in the room. If you wear a solid color that is different from the colors behind you, you will act as a color block and keep the attention on you. Also, avoid any shiny or ruffly fabrics that will make a noise or draw the eye away from you while you are speaking. And while everyone loves great jewelry and other accessories, remember that any noisy items will sound even louder on a conference call.

Alternative Setup
STYLE #7

THE BEACH HOUSE

While relatively few people own their own beach house, it is one of the most popular types of vacation and weekend rentals. The good news is that beach houses can make quite a good alternative setup; the bad news is that you're working on vacation. While few would choose to live year-round with typical beach house décor, with the exception of some Florida residents, it can be a fun break. Embrace it. You'll want dried starfish on the wall, at least one painting of a lighthouse, and a driftwood coffee table. Lobster-trap end tables are perfect. Collections of shells and shades of blue conjure up visions of seaside holidays and the smell of salt water.

Clutter

LARRY SABATO RENOWNED POLITICAL SCIENTIST

How much is too much? There's a continuum from spare to comfortable to cozy to cluttered.

SPARE. This is not Scandinavian or European modernism, nor deliberate minimalism with clean lines. This is a room with not enough stuff in it. If there were any less in it, we'd call it a hostage video. It won't look good on camera. You need more.

COMFORTABLE. This is where most of us plan to be. Sometimes we fall short and sometimes we overdo it, but this is where most of us will end up if we put a little effort into our room setup. You have enough furniture, art, maybe plants and books. Something to make the room your own. Stop there.

COZY. Rarely a goal but often a destination. This is where my aunt Vicky is. Not that cozy equals age, but it would be foolish to say there's no correlation. In truth, a lifetime well lived gives you the chance to surround yourself with a degree of familiarity and comfort. As with many things, just don't go overboard.

CLUTTERED. No one starts out by saying "I want a really cluttered space." It's usually more like falling asleep on a train. Suddenly you wake up one day and there you are. And it's a fine line. How much is too much?

Get Organized

No matter what setup style you choose for your video calls, keeping things organized is essential. The room will look tidy and uncluttered, and a small space will appear larger. Using various kinds of storage bins can really step up your organization game. These come in all shapes and sizes and materials. They can be baskets or boxes. They can fit on shelves and under furniture. They can be stacked and hidden or look cool enough to be a complement to your existing furnishings.

Shelves are a great way to organize any room. They can display your prized possessions, like books, photos, art, and plants, of course. But they can also be used for storage. This will help keep surfaces clear enough that you can put one or two well-placed decorative items on that table instead of a stack of paper or books.

We like floating shelves because they look clean and can be worked into any room décor. They also can fill empty spaces on walls, which are never attractive on-camera. Done right, they can even be works of art. They are convenient but are also functional and sturdy. If you are a DIY person, they are known to be easy to install. We have no firsthand knowledge of this, but we will take the word of others on this one. We are pro–baskets and bins to store clutter, as nicely designed baskets or bins can look great.

Desk storage is especially important if you Zoom from a home office. Make the most of your desk drawers by getting file holders, dividers, and containers. If your desktop is cleared off, you will have room to personalize it and add a small succulent.

GURDEEP PANDHER CANADIAN AMBASSADOR OF JOY

Joy is more than having fun. Joy means your nerves are calm, your anxieties are elsewhere. Your heart (not only your lips) is smiling; your breathing is soothing like a breeze; your world is perfect in the mess of imperfections around you. Joy could be an ideal meditation. If all emotions are valuable, then even tears of joy can make us get up and dance. One thing more about joy: we need it, just like we need food to survive. Go find your joy! Start by searching within yourself or going out in nature.

—Gurdeep Pandheer

Conclusion

We've all been through a lot in the last couple of years. We've known personal and collective loss, but are emerging from it with a greater sense of resiliency and determination. Our lives have been altered; how we educate our kids, how we approach work, and how we interact with friends and family have undergone dramatic change. Our goal is to make some of these realities a bit more manageable, to have some fun, and to bring a bit of joy to all of your rooms. Thank you all for being a part of it with us. Call us Room Rater. We'll be seeing you.

Acknowledgments

Wе would first and foremost like to thank our illustrator and co-creator, Chris Morris, who made this book possible and brought our vision to life.

Neither our Twitter account nor the book would have been possible without the assistance and guidance of Allan Andres, Amy Hathaway, Avi Taylor, Blair W. Carrigan, Erin Dickens, Gopalan Sridhar, Jan Lagomarsino Brummett, Joann Biondi, Liz Kearley, Mary Raichinis, and Michael Chapman. From spotting rooms to rate and doing research, to answering many questions and editing, this was truly a team effort.

We are so very grateful to our contributors, who generously donated their time and wisdom to this project, and gave us a glimpse into their rooms and lives.

We would also like to thank the following people who took a chance on us and helped us fulfill this dream: Susan Golomb and Madeline Ticknor from Writer's House; and our team at Voracious books: Ben Allen, Bonni Leon-Berman, Emma Brodie, Katherine Akey, Lauren Harms, Lauren Ortiz, Mary Tondorf-Dick, Meghan Tillett, Mike Szczerban, Nyamekye Waliyaya, and Thea Diklich-Newell.

But most of all, thank you to all of our followers.

About the Authors

Claude Taylor has worked as a professional travel photographer and a political operative. He served on Bill Clinton's White House staff. From 1998 to 2016 he also worked as a gallery owner. For the last several years he has served as chair of a political action committee, Mad Dog PAC. He currently resides in Maryland.

Jessie Bahrey has worked in telecommunications and as an editor for a PI company. She currently manages a commercial greenhouse/nursery in Port Moody, British Columbia.

Chris Morris is an award-winning illustrator based just outside Cleveland in Rocky River, Ohio. He has long worked as an editorial illustrator for a number of newspapers, and his freelance clients include the *New York Times,* the *Boston Globe,* the *Los Angeles Times, LA Magazine,* and ESPN among many others. He also teaches as an adjunct professor in the illustration department of the Columbus College of Art & Design.